IRAQ, TERROR, AND THE PHILIPPINES' WILL TO WAR

IRAQ, TERROR, AND THE PHILIPPINES' WILL TO WAR

JAMES A. TYNER

ROWMAN & LITTLEFIELD PUBLISHERS, INC.

Lanham • Boulder • New York • Toronto • Oxford

ROWMAN & LITTLEFIELD PUBLISHERS, INC.

Published in the United States of America
by Rowman & Littlefield Publishers, Inc.
A wholly owned subsidary of The Rowman & Littlefield Publishing Group, Inc.
4501 Forbes Boulevard, Suite 200, Lanham, Maryland 20706
www.rowmanlittlefield.com

P.O. Box 317, Oxford OX2 9RU, UK

British Library Cataloging in Publication Information Available

Library of Congress Cataloging-in-Publication Data

Tyner, James A., 1966–
    Iraq, terror, and the Philippines' will to war / James A. Tyner.
      p. cm.
    Includes bibliographical references and index.
    ISBN 0-7425-3860-5 (cloth: alk. paper) — ISBN 0-7425-3861-3
(pbk.: alk. paper)
      1. Philippines—Foreign relations—1973– 2. Iraq War, 2003—Participation,
Philippine. 3. War on Terrorism, 2001– I. Title.
    DS686.614.T96 2005
    956.7044'33599—dc22

                                                                   2004027382

Printed in the United States of America

⊗™ The paper used in this publication meets the minimum requirements of
American National Standard for Information Sciences—Permanence of Paper for
Printed Library Materials, ANSI/NISO Z39.48-1992.

For Jessica

CONTENTS

ACKNOWLEDGMENTS

What began as a book on labor migration quickly moved into uncharted territories. Admittedly, my interest in the subject was founded on my long-standing work in the field of migration studies. Indeed, the roots of this book can be traced to my earlier book *Made in the Philippines: Gendered Discourses and the Making of Migrants* in which I examined the discourses of Philippine international labor migration. As I completed that book (in the spring of 2003), the Philippine state was planning for the reconstruction of Iraq. The immediacy of writing this book literally required me to change trajectories on a daily basis.

I thank Derek Gregory and Colin Flint for their early encouragement in my pursuit of this research. Thanks are also owed to my current chair, Jay Lee, for his support. I am indebted to Susan McEachern, Jessica Gribble, and Jennifer Nemec at Rowman & Littlefield for their belief in this project as well as their tireless efforts of seeing this book through to completion. Over the years I have been fortunate to learn from a number of colleagues, including graduate students, faculty, and other researchers: Curt Roseman, Michael Dear, Maruja Asis, Rob Kruse, Gabe Popescue, Stuart Aitken, Nicola Piper, Graziano Battistella, Larry Brown, and Gary Peters.

A special note of gratitude is extended to Steve Oluic. In addition to reading and critiquing earlier drafts of this book, Steve provided materials and insights that I had not previously considered. For his help, I express my appreciation. Steve is a friend and a colleague; I am honored to know him.

I thank also my parents, Dr. Gerald Tyner and Dr. Judith Tyner, for their continued support and encouragement. Thanks also to my other family members, David, Floris, Karen, and Bill. And thanks are extended to my late-night companions, Bond (my puppy) and Jamaica (my cat) who stayed up with me while I wrote.

As always, it is to my wife, Belinda, to whom I owe the greatest debt—and not just for making me coffee late at night. During the writing of this book, and throughout my career as well, Belinda has stood beside me, tirelessly supporting and encouraging my work. She has tolerated my absent-mindedness, the mess of articles and books strewn across the room, and the hectic days of finishing this manuscript. Belinda has been, and remains, my inspiration, my rock, my friend. My deepest thanks, though, must be for the strength, patience, and guidance of her in the raising of our daughter Jessica. *Maraming salamat.* And it is to Jessica that I dedicate this book.

Autumn is fast approaching, and Jessica is asleep in her bed. She is just twenty-three months of age; her days are spent playing at the park, and visiting the zoo. Jessica especially likes tigers. She does not yet know of war and terror. And I am unsure how I will explain these to her in the years to come. Perhaps this book will provide some understanding. My hope, ultimately, is that in the years to come, Jessie, and all children, *will be able* to visit tigers at the zoo.

1

GLOBAL CONSTRUCTIONS

And all that believed were together,
and had all things common.

Acts 2:44

On May 20, 2003, on the South Lawn of the White House, Philippine President Gloria Macapagal-Arroyo discussed the necessity of standing firm against terrorism, of not accommodating, although the temptation is great. She explained that it was crucial for the Philippines and the United States to remain firm in their alliance because "in the face of terror the temptation to disengage is strong. We must fight that temptation, because the answer to fear is confrontation. Indeed, we must close ranks and stand firm against terrorist threats, however grave, however armed, and from whatever quarter." Indicating the Philippines' commitment as a member of the coalition, Macapagal-Arroyo continued, "To space themselves, some countries might prefer an accommodation with terrorism. The Philippines has chosen to fight terrorism. We compensate for such modern means as we command with an unshakable resolve to defeat terrorism once and for all, and with faith in the justice of our cause and our friendship with the United States."[1]

Fourteen months later, however, that "unshakable resolve" collapsed. In July 2004 a Filipino truck driver was abducted while working in Iraq. He was one of many foreign workers who, in the aftermath of the Iraqi War, was held hostage in an attempt to pressure foreign governments to pull troops out of the region. After days of speculation and ambiguous press statements, the Philippine president made a startling decision. She agreed to the demands of the abductors and ordered the withdrawal of the Philippines' contingent of peacekeepers. Her decision infuriated many officials in the United States and elsewhere, including Australia and Singapore. In the eyes of her critics, the president appeared to accommodate terrorism, a decision that could significantly damage the relationship between the Philippines and the United States.

How are we to interpret the Philippines' initial and overwhelming support for the "Coalition of the Willing"? Was the foreign policy of the Philippines determined simply by coercive international leverage, or were other components at stake? And why after twenty-two months did the Macapagal-Arroyo administration apparently waver in its commitment to the coalition? Was it a lack of resolve in the "War on Terror" as some commentators suggest? Or again, might other factors account for this turn of events?

This is a study of the Philippines' foreign policy for a brief but substantial moment in history. Situated within the events surrounding the American-led invasion and occupation of Iraq as well as the larger U.S.-led War on Terror, I examine the discourses and material practices that undergirded the Philippines' participation as a member of the coalition. The significance of this investigation, however, surpasses this singular case study, for I make the argument that, through an understanding of the Philippines' "Will to War," other insights into international coalition-building may be developed.

Compared to the attention paid to European states—especially Germany, France, and Russia—little sustained interest has been directed toward nonmajor participants in the Bush administration's Coalition of the Willing. When combat operations began in March 2003, the Bush administration counted forty-six countries as having committed to the coalition. Not all participants agreed to provide combat troops; contributions also, or primarily, included logistical and intelligence support, specialized chemical and biological response teams, overflight rights, and humanitarian and reconstruction support.

Spokespersons for the United States used these countries as political resources, indicating a global support for war. Secretary of State Colin Powell expressed his optimism, noting, "I've seen this repeatedly in the course of my career when war was at hand, and it takes strong leaders who understand the danger and understand the importance of dealing with an issue like this." Powell continued, "It takes those kinds of leaders to come together and stand tall as they are now standing tall in this coalition of 30 plus 15 more who we will know in due course."[2] Likewise, Pentagon spokesperson Marine Lieutenant Colonel Mike Humm explained that "the fact that

45 countries are involved helps point out what we've been saying all along—that U.S. actions are not unilateral."[3]

Or does it? Critics of the Bush administration have asserted that the Coalition of the Willing is more aptly described as a "Coalition of the Coerced." A report distributed by the Institute for Policy Studies, for example, suggests that many governments have supported the U.S.-led campaigns against Iraq "only through coercion, bullying, bribery, or the implied threat of U.S. action."[4] Critics identify that most members of the coalition are politically impotent players on the global stage: Iceland, the Marshall Islands, Mongolia, Palau, Rwanda, the Solomon Islands. Support for American foreign policies is exchanged for economic assistance or military protection—including protection from the United States.

While I am sympathetic to critics of the Bush administration—namely, that the United States, by dint of its economic and military superiority, is able to forward its own agenda through bribes and threats—I am concerned that we may too readily ignore the decision-making capability of "peripheral" states. I do not discount the multiple leverages of the United States, but at the same time I do not discount the agency (however limited) of other sovereign governments. Indeed, we may read the actions of these governments as forming a "Coalition of the Opportunists." History is replete with examples of territorial acquisitions by peripheral governments in the aftermath of major military operations. It may very well be, therefore, that some of the forty-six members of the coalition sought to benefit in ways far removed from American policies.

Consequently, to reduce the actions of certain members, the Philippines, for example, risks obfuscating more than it reveals, owing to an a priori relation of dependency and subservience. Indeed, in the course of my argument I suggest that, at one level, the Philippines did willingly participate in the Coalition of the Willing. That segments of the Philippines—chiefly the military—stood to gain by joining the coalition should not be seen as overriding other interests forwarded by the Macapagal-Arroyo administration.

This book provides one such alternative interpretation of the coalition. Two premises guide my overall argument. First, as will be evident, the foreign policy of the Philippines is intimately connected with overseas employment. The Philippines is the world's largest exporter of government-sponsored overseas contract labor migration; annually, over seven hundred thousand workers are deployed to over 190 countries and territories on either six-month or two-year contracts. The deployment of labor is also hotly contested. Indeed, critics of the Philippines' overseas employment program claim that the government is sacrificing its workers for profit. The experience of highly publicized cases of migrant death and abuse has added to the opposition to the export of labor. Accordingly, within the last decade, the Philippine government has adopted various discourses to justify, rationalize, and legitimate its contentious policies. That these two components—foreign policy and overseas employment—are inseparable is made clear in numerous documents disseminated by the Philippines' Department of Foreign Affairs as well as its Office of the President.

Second, foreign policies as forwarded by the Macapagal-Arroyo administration are guided by a Catholic political fundamentalism. David Domke defines *political fundamentalism* as an intertwining of conservative religious faith, politics, and strategic communication. According to Domke, after the terrorist attacks of September 11, 2001, the Bush administration forwarded a particular worldview that had deep and conservative Christian roots yet felt political—and thus was received favorably by the U.S. public. By extension, I believe that this political fundamentalism resonated strongly with Macapagal-Arroyo, a devout Roman Catholic who has explicitly attempted to shape the foreign policies of the Philippines to conform more readily with Scripture.[5]

CONSTRUCTING MEANINGS

Discourse is a widely used but rarely defined term in the political literature. In this book, *discourse* refers not to disembodied collections of statements but rather groupings of statements that are produced within a particular context. Discourses are thus derived from statements, and these statements have a material existence; they have a substance in that they are manifest in particular places and specific times (e.g., in the form of speeches, policies, or press statements). Statements, however, do not have as correlate an individual or particular object. In other words, there is no "true" referent to statements or to discourses. Indeed, following the work of the French social theorist Michel Foucault, discourses are seen as practices that systematically form the objects of which they speak. This is crucial in that it is through discourse that migration, globalization, and indeed the War on Terror are produced. As I argue elsewhere, discourses of migration do not speak *of* migrants but rather *produce* migrants as objects.[6] This is not to discount the material existence of bodies moving across space (e.g., migration) but rather highlights the idea that the meaning of migration is discursively produced. Thus, it is through discourse that some bodies are labeled "refugees" while others are classified as "undocumented aliens." In like fashion, the distinction between a member of the Coalition of the Willing or the "Axis of Evil" or between a "soldier" or a "terrorist" is discursively produced.

Philosophically, therefore, I follow the work of geographers, political scientists, and international relations scholars who incorporate poststructuralism into their studies. There is no single definition of *poststructuralism*, although the term generally refers to a collection of theories or perspectives based on the writings of Michel Foucault, Jacques Derrida, and Roland Barthes, among others. Language is paramount in poststructural approaches; epistemologically, poststructuralists ask fundamental questions about the meaning and subjectivity. Poststructural approaches disrupt meanings, labels, and categories; in other words, poststructuralism challenges terms that are assumed to be natural and unchanging. Poststructural epistemology, furthermore, permanently troubles the notion that there can be a direct relationship between objects and the meanings they denote. A poststructural political geography, as explained by Paul Reuber, elucidates the central role that language plays in the preparation of physical violence—combat. Consequently, geopolitics becomes a "war of discourse on space, power and politics. It is the instrument not only to define Good and Evil, but also to locate and confine such stereotypes in space, creating different territories separating between 'us' and them.'"[7] These spaces may be those of the Coalition of the Willing, the Axis of Evil, or even "rogue" states and states that harbor terrorists. In *Iraq, Terror, and the Philippines' Will to War,* I highlight the intertextuality of these discursive spaces. As Foucault explained, "There is no statement in general, no free, neutral, independent statement; but a statement always belongs to a series or a whole, always plays a role among other statements, deriving support from them and distinguishing itself from them: it is always part of a network of statements."[8] This sentiment is captured by the concept of *intertextuality*, a term introduced by literary theorist Julia Kristeva. Intertextuality suggests that the meanings of any one text (e.g., Executive Order 194) depend not only on that one source but also on the meanings carried by other texts (e.g., Bush's State of the Union address or the *National Security Strategy of the United States*).

Such a discursive understanding is vital to a study of the coalition-building activities surrounding the occupation of Iraq and the larger War on Terror. As Gordon Clark and Michael Dear write, social reality is structured through political language.[9] Murray Edelman elaborates, noting that it is language about political events rather than the events themselves that everyone experiences.[10] As such, in this work I concur with Eve Sedgwick, whose main strategy in her research has been repeatedly to ask how certain categorizations work, what enactments they are performing, and what they are creating rather than what they essentially mean.[11] To this end, my primary focus is on the political language that constructed (and later deconstructed) the Philippines' participation in the Coalition of the Willing.

This chapter is entitled "Global Constructions," for in it I emphasize the myriad meanings of *construction*. On one hand, the term refers to the rebuilding efforts—the physical reconstruction of a war-torn country—of foreign labor following military conflict. Consider, though, the following events. In the 1980s Filipino contract workers built the secret tunnels of Saddam Hussein; these tunnels, subsequently, were targeted by U.S. military forces during their invasion of Iraq in 2003. Consider also that Filipino (and Asian-Indian) contract workers constructed the detention camps on Guantanamo Bay in Cuba to hold alleged terrorists captured during the 2001–2002 U.S. military intervention in Afghanistan. And following the 2003 invasion, the Philippine government positioned itself to capitalize on the rebuilding of Iraq.

On the other hand, *construction* also refers to the use of political language to garner support for controversial actions. This is manifest in the construction of military intervention by states as "just" or "moral." These justifications, likewise, are strongly associated with the discursive framing of other peoples and places. The declaration of Iraq, Iran, and North Korea as part of an Axis of Evil represents just one recent construction.

The most prominent construction, of course, is that of the Coalition of the Willing. All international alliances are political constructions and the U.S.-led coalition leading up to the war in Iraq was no exception. During late 2002 and early 2003 the Bush administration attempted to convince the United Nations Security Council to authorize war on Iraq. The Security Council is combined of fifteen states—five "permanent members" (China, France, Russia, the United Kingdom, and the United States) who hold veto power and ten "nonpermanent" members (Bulgaria, Spain, Guinea, Cameroon, Angola, Mexico, Chile, Pakistan, Germany, and Syria); these nonpermanent members are elected by the General Assembly and serve two-year terms. During the lead-up to war, it became increasingly clear that the United States would not receive UN authorization for war: a council resolution requires nine positive votes and no veto to pass. Germany and France were strongly opposed to a UN authorization for war. Accordingly, the Bush administration, with the United Kingdom, had to construct a Coalition of the Willing to provide legitimacy for a non–UN-sanctioned war. In actuality, preparations for the coalition began as early as January 2002. The Bush administration was determined to bring about war in Iraq.

Within the realm of international relations as each state pursues its own goals, other states become relevant only to the extent that they represent opportunities for, or constraints on, goal achievement. The U.S.–led war on Iraq was largely a unilateral mission. However, even the most militarily dominant state must rely on contributions from other states. This may include the provision of troops; equally important, however, are considerations of overflight rights, access to seaways, and staging grounds for land troops. Perhaps more important for the Bush administration was the symbolic function of a coalition. Without UN support, it was politically astute—though not a requirement—to demonstrate global support for military intervention.

If we assume that the Coalition of the Willing was constructed by the United States in an attempt to forward its own agenda, the question is begged: Why should other states, such as the Philippines, join the coalition? No doubt the gauntlet-throwing threat enunciated by Bush that "you're either with us or against us" played into the foreign policy considerations of some states. We may assume, also, that other states would view an alliance with the United States as serving ulterior motives, such as economic or military aid. In general, though, there are three forms of leverage, none of which are mutually exclusive, that states may attempt to employ in their international relations. Military leverage consists of both positive and negative forms. On the positive side, states may provide military assistance in the form of protection, provision of military resources, and training. Negative military leverage implies the use or threat of military action against a state. Given the "us or them" attitude of the United States, the implied threat certainly could not be ruled out. Economic leverage is used when states manipulate the actions of other states through the imposition of unequal trade agreements, tariffs, or the imposition of sanctions. Lastly, political leverage is derived from the ability of a state to affect the actions of other states by the application of political resources, its control of political institutions, or its overall influence in international relations. The United States, for example, maintains essentially a "veto" on states attempting to join the North Atlantic Treaty Organization (NATO). It is not coincidental, therefore, that several states that supported U.S. military action in Iraq are attempting to become members of NATO, such as Albania, Bulgaria, Estonia, Latvia, Lithuania, Macedonia, Romania, Slovakia, and Slovenia.[12]

In general, the Philippines' support for the U.S.-led war in Iraq has been explained based on perceived benefits. As Sarah Anderson and her colleagues write, the Philippines is dependent on the U.S. government for both economic and military assistance, and indeed, the country received

$71 million in USAID (U.S. Agency for International Development) money in 2002. Equally important for these scholars was the fact that the Philippines was waging an ongoing struggle against Islamic separatist groups.[13] Therefore, military assistance in the form of weapons and American troops for "training" exercises would be a welcome reward for joining the coalition.

To reduce the Philippines' participation as simply resultant of U.S. leverage, however, is unsatisfactory. Indeed, Philippine officials viewed the reconstruction effort as affording many more possibilities than simple U.S. economic and military assistance. Consider, for example, that on April 15, 2003, as U.S. Pentagon officials indicated that major military operations were over, Macapagal-Arroyo signed Executive Orders 194 and 195. Combined, these two orders provided for the formation of a public–private sector task force to coordinate Philippine participation in the postwar reconstruction of Iraq. Philippine government officials planned to deploy thirty thousand to one hundred thousand Filipino contract workers. Thus, the connections between foreign policy and overseas employment emerge as a crucial component. This consideration did not go unnoticed, however, as numerous politicians and critics in the Philippines chastised the Macapagal-Arroyo administration for sending workers to capitalize on war.

But even this explanation falls short, and it is for this reason I emphasize the idea of the Philippines' Will to War. This phrase is in obvious reference to the idea of "God's will." Within the Christian tradition, the term *God's will* has many usages. It refers to God's eternal plan or, alternatively, to God's desire or consent. Crucial for my purpose is the use of *God's will* in reference to making difficult choices. This usage is found, for example, in the book of Exodus when Moses tells his father-in-law, "Because the people come to me to seek God's will. Whenever they have a dispute, it is brought to me, and I decide between the parties and inform them of God's decrees and laws" (Exodus 18:15–16). God's will is thus sought to provide guidance and certainty in times of crisis. As will become clear in chapters 3 and 4, both Macapagal-Arroyo and Bush refer to their doing God's will. However, fundamental differences will become apparent, and it is these differences that account for the shift in the Philippines' foreign policy. In short, the Philippines' decision to participate in both the U.S.-led War on Terror and the subsequent invasion of Iraq was based on the Catholic-informed political fundamentalism of Macapagal-Arroyo. And in this respect, the moral politics of the Philippine president intersect with the political fundamentalism of Bush. Between September 2001 and July 2004 the interests of Macapagal-Arroyo were consonant with those of the Bush administration—

namely, the humanitarian fight against terrorism, poverty, and the forward-ing of human rights. However, I suggest that by July 2004 the *beliefs* of Macapagal-Arroyo became increasingly discordant with those of the Bush administration. Her decision to go against the United States—and, crucially, *not* the principles of the Coalition of the Willing—therefore signifies an im-portant stand against an imperial superpower. Such is the terrain I attempt to traverse in the chapters to come. In the remainder of this chapter, how-ever, I provide a brief overview of the Philippines, with a special emphasis on Philippine president Gloria Macapagal-Arroyo.

THE PHILIPPINES

In March 2003, the U.S. State Department identified approximately forty-six members of the Coalition of the Willing. By the summer of 2004, member-ship had dwindled to about thirty-two members. Support among many gov-ernments appeared to be waning, particularly in the face of increased acts of violence perpetrated toward foreign nationals working in postwar Iraq. The decision of the Philippines to remove its peacekeeping contingent, however, was viewed as a significant blow to the appearance of global solidarity. For this reason alone the Philippines' foreign policy merits attention.

The Philippines has also been identified as a crucial node in Southeast Asia—dubbed the "Second Front" in the War on Terror. Home of two long-established separatist groups—the Moro National Liberation Front and the Moro Islamic Liberation Front—as well as the more recently formed Abu Sayyaf Group, the Philippines is also believed to be a primary training ground for other Islamic extremist groups, such as Jemaah Islamiyah.

The Philippines is an archipelago composed of approximately seventy-one hundred islands. Only about one thousand of these islands, however, are populated, and just eleven islands constitute 94 percent of the landmass that makes up the Philippines. Stretching north to south, the geography of the Philippines is arranged into three major island groupings. Luzon is the largest, most populous island and with the capital of Manila is the political and economic center of power. The Visayan Islands, which include Cebu and Leyte, encompass the central Philippines. The southern Philippines is dominated by the large island of Mindanao and numerous smaller islands, including the Sulu Island chain stretching toward Malaysia.

There was no unified "Philippines" before European colonization, nor was there a unifying precolonial empire of kingdom in existence as was present in other parts of Southeast Asia. Instead, a system of local Islamic sultanates and other fiefdoms ruled by local chiefs typified the precolonial archipelago. As such, the Philippines is often described as beginning with the arrival of foreigners: Chinese and Arab traders, Islamic missionaries, and Spanish *conquistadores*.

The Philippines were colonized and Christianized by Spain beginning in the sixteenth century. Initiated by the voyage of the Portugese navigator Ferdinand Magellan (sailing under the Spanish flag) and sustained by Spaniards such as Legazpi, the purpose of Spanish colonialism was to gain access to immediate riches via a twofold strategy: first, assume entrée into the spice trades; second, link to a lucrative China market. These objectives were only marginally met. There was no instant wealth to be found, certainly not on the order of Spain's conquests in central America. And over time, the Philippines—though, principally Manila—emerged as a nodal point in the galleon trades linking China with Spain's American empire. Consequently, the extent and effect of Spanish colonialism throughout the archipelago was uneven, both in terms of geographic scope and administrative control. Three legacies of this period continue to affect contemporary society. First, the Philippines' economy remains oriented toward the selling of primary products on the world market. This includes the "selling" of labor. Second, colonialism led to the formation of an elite social class with a vested interest in continued outside involvement. And third, the colonial experience produced a profound and yet partial absorption of European practices, beliefs, and ideals. Under Spanish colonialism, Filipinos became Hispanicized: the population became devout, if somewhat syncretic, Catholics.[14]

In 1898 the United States acquired the Philippines as part of the spoils of the Spanish-American War. America's decision to colonize the Philippines was shaped by a prolonged and hesitant evolution of U.S. policy in both the Caribbean and the Pacific following the consolidation of its continental boundaries. American colonial expansion in the Pacific throughout the nineteenth century was gradual, marked by Commodore Matthew Perry's "opening" of Japan and the possession of dozens of remote islands in the Pacific, including the Hawaiian Islands and parts of Samoa. Many of these territorial acquisitions were the result of an enlarged maritime presence of the United States, especially as it was related with both the whaling industry and the strengthening U.S. Navy.

Crucially, the American colonization of the Philippines was also influenced by a broader international environment of imperial capitalist expansion, as the industrializing powers of northwest Europe competed for colonies throughout Africa and Asia. Within the United States, imperialists such as Henry Cabot Lodge and Alfred Thayer Mahan advocated for a strong American presence abroad. Extending the idea of America's "manifest destiny," the imperialists argued that only as a world power could the United States trade, prosper, and protect itself against potential enemies.[15]

America's colonization of the Philippines was far from bloodless. Indeed, the U.S. imperialists found themselves confronting an established Filipino revolution, one that had spent the previous years attempting to overthrow Spanish domination. The Philippine-American War (1899–1902) saw battle losses of over forty-two hundred Americans killed and over twenty-eight hundred wounded. For the Filipinos, between sixteen thousand and twenty thousand died in combat; an estimated two hundred thousand "innocent" Filipinos died of famine, disease, and other war-related calamities.[16]

After decades of Spanish neglect and the subsequent destructive war to subdue the Filipinos, the United States embarked on a period of colonial reconstruction. It was President William McKinley who coined the term *benevolent assimilation* to define America's occupation of the archipelago. But whether defined as liberators or tutors, the American occupation of the Philippines was, at its core, a colonial project. Veiled by racist imagery of uplifting the Filipino people—the first U.S. civilian governor of the Philippines, William Howard Taft, condescendingly referred to them as America's "little brown brothers"—American policy focused on remaking the Philippines and its citizens. English became the medium of communication, binding the disparate linguistic, geographic, and religious constituencies. U.S. education was to train Filipinos to be good colonial subjects, conforming to American ideas.[17]

Economically, however, American businesses were given a virtual import monopoly. This practice, in effect, stunted the growth of Philippine industry and preserved the archipelago as an agricultural society. Following independence in 1946, through a series of unequal treaties, this pattern was reimposed, thereby maintaining the Philippines in a subservient neocolonial economic relationship with the United States. Politically, a patron–client system was established. Unlike other colonial powers, however, the United States was exceptionally liberal in its approach to political rights in its territories. Thus, although the right to vote was restricted to the educated class, many Filipinos were allowed to participate in politics. As early as 1907, the Philippines had its own national legislature—the first in Asia. Over time, however, many Filipino politicians would owe their political lives to American patronage before and after independence, such as the first president of the Philippine Commonwealth, Sergio Osmeña, and more recent presidents, such as Ramon Magsaysay and Ferdinand Marcos.

The incipient political relationship of the United States and the Philippines, though, was manifest within a patron–client style relationship, one that Anthony Woodiwiss terms *mendicant patriarchalism*.[18] *Patriarchalism* refers to "a familialist discourse that, regardless of the institutional context, both assumes the naturalness of inequalities in the social relations between people and justifies these by reference to the respect due to a benevolent father or father-figure who exercises a 'joint right.'" *Mendicant* means "begging," and it has been used in the Philippine literature to denote the debased form of patriarchalist practice that has become the established mode of exercising power within the society—political leaders, before and after independence, begging Americans for favors so that the former could in turn respond to others who were begging for favors.[19] I argue that the Philippine government's acquiesce to U.S. foreign policy, as well as its rush to be identified as a member of the Coalition of the Willing, may partially be understood through the lens of mendicant patriarchalism.

Although the War on Terror and the subsequent U.S.–led invasion and occupation of Iraq will serve as defining issues for the international relations of the Philippines for the twenty-first century, the decision of Philippine president Macapagal-Arroyo to agree to the demands of the Iraqi hostage takers will leave the most striking legacy. Three factors are prominent. First, the Philippines is highly dependent on the Middle East as a destination for overseas employment. In 2002 alone the Philippine government deployed 306,939 workers to the Middle East. Saudi Arabia was the largest recipient of Filipino workers, registering 193,157 of them, with the United Arab Emirates (50,796), Kuwait (25,894), Qatar (11,516), and Bahrain (6,034) rounding out the top five Middle Eastern destinations. Second, the Philippines remains dependent on the Middle East. Every Philippine president from the time of Ferdinand Marcos through the present administration of Macapagal-Arroyo has been keenly aware of the need to propitiate Middle Eastern oil producers. Third, the Philippine state is confronted with ongoing negotiations and civil war with Muslim separatists in the southern part of the archipelago. As discussed in the following, the emergence and existence of the insurgent Communist Party of the Philippines and three Muslim separatist groups—the Moro National Liberation Front, the Moro Islamic Liberation Front, and, more recently, the Abu Sayyaf Group—form arguably the most significant policy issue confronting the Philippine state, one that intersects in complex ways both domestically and internationally. On one hand, Islamic separatist groups in the Philippines receive financial backing, training, and other forms of assistance from other Islamic states in both Southeast Asia and the Middle East. Many of the "fighters" associated with the Abu Sayyaf Group, for example, trained and fought in the wars in Afghanistan. On the other hand, Muslim separatism is intimately associated with oil dependence and labor conditions for Filipino contract workers.[20] The Communist Party of the Philippines in some ways operates as a wild card in these developments.

To sum, the Philippine government's attempt to capitalize on the rebuilding of Iraq has therefore contributed to a multitude of geopolitical tensions, domestically, regionally, and internationally. By aligning itself as part of America's Coalition of the Willing, the Philippine government finds itself at risk of alienating itself from its Muslim neighbors. Since the early weeks following the September 11 attacks, Southeast Asia has been viewed—by politicians inside and outside of the region—as the "second front in the war on terror," a point reiterated by spokespersons of the fifty-seven-member-state Organization of Islamic Conference (OIC). In October of 2003, for example, OIC Secretary-General Abdelouahed Belkeziz announced that the Muslim world faced dangers in the War on Terror: "We are now faced with a new world reality where Islam, Muslims and their values have become objects of discredit, and some Muslim countries targets of antagonism." He continued that "accusations of religious bigotry and the culture of violence are also leveled against Islamic civilization. We are also accused of rejecting the principles and values of democracy, the rule of law, human rights and good governance."[21] Macapagal-Arroyo, who attended the tenth annual conference held in Kuala Lumpur, just days after meeting personally with President Bush, addressed the OIC with her affirmation of support of the Islamic world for peace and development in Mindanao.

MUSLIM SEPARATIST GROUPS

Introduced by Arab merchants and Islamic missionaries, Islam diffused to the southern Philippines by way of present-day Indonesia as early as 1210. Resistance to subsequent interference by "foreigners" has been strong among the Philippine Muslim population. Throughout the Spanish colonial period (1521–1898) and the American period (1898–1946), for example, Muslim Filipinos fought against both Christian and foreign domination. Crucially, many of these former clashes continue to resonate in the demands of contemporary separatist movements.

Those Islamic separatist groups currently active in the Philippines claim historical precedence to their ultimate demands of territorial sovereignty. The groups cite the fact that, first, Spain was never able to subjugate the preexisting Islamic sultanates that were established throughout Mindanao and the Sulu Islands. Indeed, by the time of Spain's arrival in the early sixteenth century, three Islamic sultanates had been founded in southern Philippines: the Sulu Sultanate (which included Basilan, Tawi-Tawi, Palawan, and a handful of neighboring islands), the Sultanate of Maguindanao, and the Confederated Sultanates of Ranao.

Second, these groups refer to past treaties that allegedly promise sovereignty. Three treaties in particular stand out. In July 1878 the Spanish Treaty of Peace was signed by Spanish authorities and the Sultan of Sulu. Crucially, scholars fluent in Spanish and Arabic have determined that serious translation flaws exist in the treaty. According to the Spanish version, Spain assumed sovereignty over Sulu; conversely, the Tausug version established a protectorate relationship rather than a dependency relationship. The treaty, additionally, indicates that the customs, laws, and religion of the Muslim peoples would not be subjected to Spanish jurisdiction.

Two decades of Spanish rule in the Philippines came to an abrupt end, only to be replaced by American occupying forces. On December 10, 1898, in the aftermath of the Spanish–American War, the Treaty of Paris was signed. According to this treaty, Spain ceded to the United States the territories of Cuba, Puerto Rico, Guam, and the Philippines. In return, the United States paid $20 million to the Spanish for the Philippines. Crucially, the treaty included all of the Islamic-controlled regions of the Philippines, despite the fact that Spain did not exercise sovereignty over these territories.

American officials did not make contact with the Sultanates in the southern Philippines until May 1899. When they arrived in Jolo, they informed the Sultan of Sulu, Jamalul Kiram II, that the United States had taken over Spain's possession and asked the Sultan to recognize the United States in the place of Spain. The Sultan was also asked to recognize the provisions of the 1878 treaty. At this point the Sultan refused, believing that a new treaty was in order, given the departure of Spain. In place of the earlier treaty, the Sultan proposed a sixteen-point treaty; included among the provisions was the clause that the United States could not occupy any land without the permission of the Sultan. Brigadier General John Bates, the U.S. official in charge, rejected the Sultan's proposal on the grounds that it refused to recognize U.S. sovereignty.

Bates countered the Sultan's offer with his own fifteen-point proposal. Included in the Bates proposal was the guarantee of noninterference with the Islamic religion and customs and a pledge that the United States would not sell the island of Jolo or any other island of the Sulu Archipelago to any foreign nation without the consent of the Sultan. In the end, the Sultan agreed, and on August 20, 1899, the Bates Treaty was signed.

Within five years, however, the United States unilaterally ended the Bates Treaty. The cause of the abrogation is itself contested. According to U.S. officials, the Sultan was unable to halt Muslim resistance to American occupying forces. It was claimed that the treaty was also a hindrance to effective American control of the area. In 1914, Frank Carpenter, the U.S. governor of the Department of Mindanao and Sulu, wrote that "all the first-class agricultural land remaining in the public domain [that are still] available for acquisition . . . is to be found in Mindanao and Sulu." Resettlement of Christians to the south had begun as early as 1912.[22]

Freed from the treaty, U.S. forces embarked on a campaign—one that lasted thirteen years—to subjugate the Muslim Filipinos. The memories of this violent period of Philippine history permeate current discussions of independence. Itself a continuation of the Philippine-American War (1899–1902), the Moro Wars inflicted a heavy loss of life on the Filipino population as well as on the American forces. Using tactics and rhetoric developed during the Indian wars, U.S. military forces were required to subjugate a people who laid claim to national independence. The Filipinos, in turn, had no hope of militarily defeating the American forces in open battle and thus utilized guerrilla tactics and acts of "terror" in an attempt to protract the war, thereby causing the American public to demand that its troops come home. This tactic, incidentally, was used by the Vietnamese against the United States (1954–1975) and, apparently, Iraqi "rebels" following the 2003 war.

Both the better-known Philippine-American War and the lesser-known Moros War were marked by atrocities. During the first war, for example, General Jacob Smith led a military campaign on the island of Samar. Reports indicate that he demanded that his troops make the island "a howling wilderness." In the aftermath of a court-martial hearing centered on a marine major, it was revealed that General Smith gave the order to "kill and burn and the more you kill and burn, the better you will please me."[23] During the war, presented as a conflict between Muslims and Christians, there occurred a number of massacres that continue to inform Islamic separatists. In 1906 at Bud Dajo and later, in 1913, at Bud Bagsak, hundreds of Filipino men, women, and children were killed. These massacres were the subject of numerous articles written by Mark Twain and other members of the U.S. Anti-Imperialist League, an organization opposed to the annexation of the Philippines.

Throughout the American occupation of the Philippines (1898–1946), Muslim leaders made repeated demands requesting independence from the embryonic Philippine state. In 1921, for example, leaders objected to the proposed incorporation of the southern Philippines into an independent Philippine state; indeed, in 1924 there was a call that the islands of Mindanao, Sulu, and Palawan be made into an unorganized territory of the United States. A different proposal requested that if the southern Philippines were to be incorporated into an independent Philippine state, then in fifty years a plebiscite should be held to vote whether the territory should be incorporated into the Philippines or become an independent state. In 1946, however, when the Philippines received its independence from the United States, the whole of the southern Philippines became part of the larger, Catholic-dominated Philippine Republic. The United States used the abrogated Bates Treaty as justification for the incorporation of the southern islands.

Demands for separatism have not been based solely on historical claims. Rather, unfair social, economic, and political practices undertaken during the American colonial period and following independence have contributed to tensions. Beginning as early as 1913, for example, American authorities encouraged the migration of Christian Filipinos to the southern islands in an attempt to "civilize" the Muslim Filipinos. These migratory movements were associated with larger attempts by the United States to establish agricultural colonies. The commonwealth government of the Philippines, beginning in 1935, was likewise interested in the development of Mindanao for benefit of the "nation" and to provide for impoverished farmers. No effort was made, however, to provide for Muslim families. And perhaps most egregious, following World War II, in an attempt to suppress the Huk rebellion, the Philippine government introduced a resettlement program. According to this policy, Huk rebels and supporters were given access to land in the southern Philippines. By 1960 there were approximately ninety-three thousand migrants in the region. Government services, as well as land, were preferentially allocated. By 1970, these programs magnified profound economic disparities between Muslim and Christian communities.[24]

In the 1960s, a movement emerged that forwarded the concept of *Bangsamoro*. Derived from the words *bangsa* (nation) and *Moro,* the term refers to the collective identity of the Muslim peoples of Mindanao, Basilan, Palawan, and the Sulu and Tawi-Tawi island groupings in the southern Philippines. *Moro*, a pejorative term used by Christians and the former colonial administrations, has been reappropriated by Muslims in the Philippines. Reflecting a right of self-determination, intellectuals came to reject their ascribed hyphenated identities as Muslim Filipinos. It was within this context that the Islamic separatist movements originated.

An early organization was the Muslim Independence Movement (MIM), established in May 1968. Its formal goal was to secede from the Philippines and establish an Islamic state. Although never a popular movement, the MIM was an important forerunner to subsequent organizations, particularly the Moro National Liberation Front (MNLF). The perceived anti-Muslim strategy of the state contributed to the formation in 1968 of the MNLF, a separatist movement with full independence as the stated objective but with a more immediate goal of increased autonomy.[25] One of the initial founders was Nur Misuari, a Muslim student educated in Manila who, ironically, was a benefactor of an "assimilationist" program instituted by the Philippine government. In 1957 the Commission on National Integration was formed. One component of this commission was the provision of scholarships for Filipino Muslim students. Radicalized by the revolutionary rhetoric of Manila, Misuari directed his political goals along the lines of Muslim nationalism rather than adopting a specifically Islamic discourse.

During the first few years of its existence, the MNLF was relatively peaceful in its activities. However, as indicated in chapter 2, martial law was declared by President Marcos in 1972. Although evidence now suggests that Marcos used martial law as a means of retaining power—his presidential term limit had expired—Marcos claimed that the declaration was needed to suppress the armed conflict between Christians and Muslims as well as communist insurgencies. Accordingly, Marcos moved to suppress the MNLF by requiring Muslims in the south to surrender their firearms. Increased military intervention led to an unprecedented level of violence and disruption in the southern Philippines.

At the height of the conflict, around 1973–1975, the military arm of the MNLF, the Bangsa Moro Army, had a force of approximately thirty thousand soldiers. Of significance is the fact that during the conflict, the MNLF received support from other Islamic states, including Libya and Malaysia. Separatist groups in the Philippines continue to receive support—in various forms—from foreign governments.

In late 1976, under the auspices of the OIC, talks began between the Philippine government and representatives of the MNLF. Eventually, in 1976 an agreement was reached and signed in Tripoli providing for a cease fire and Moro autonomy in the southern Philippines. In 1987, under the administration of Corazon Aquino, the MNLF signed an agreement indicating that it would replace its goal of independence for Muslim regions with that of autonomy. Later, in 1996, this goal became reality when an agreement was finalized with the Philippine government (now under the administration of President Fidel V. Ramos). The Autonomous Region of Muslim Mindanao was formally established.

Since the 1970s, various groups have splintered off from the MNLF or have emerged separate from the MNLF. The most important splinter group remains the Moro Islamic Liberation Front (MILF). Led by Salamat Hashim, this group emerged, in part, as a result of ideological differences within the MNLF. In December 1977 a group of MNLF leaders petitioned for the resignation of Nur Misuari, the long-standing chairperson of the group. The challenge to Misuari was based largely on a perception that the leadership of the MNLF was influenced too much by Marxist ideology rather than Islamic teachings. The MILF refuses to abide the peace agreements pursued by the MNLF. Consequently, the peace negotiations and the military campaigns to suppress the MILF have continued.

The Abu Sayyaf Group (ASG) is the most recent Islamic separatist group to emerge in the Philippines. Established in the late 1990s, the ASG, whose name translates as "bearer of the sword," has rapidly developed a reputation for extreme acts of violence. Within the last decade, the ASG has carried out bombings, assassinations, and extortions. It is most known, however, for its kidnapping and attendant executions of hostages. In May 2001 the ASG kidnapped three U.S. citizens and seventeen Filipinos from a resort in Palawan. Several of the hostages were killed by the abductors; two hostages died in a rescue attempt in 2002.

Founded in Basilan Province, the ASG operates mainly in the southern Philippines and neighboring islands in Malaysia. The group is largely self-financed, supported by ransom and extortion activities. Philippine and U.S. sources indicate, however, that the ASG may receive funding from Islamic groups in the Middle East and South Asia. The ASG does have connections with al Qaeda that date to the group's founding. Organized by Abdurajak Janjalani, a former member of MNLF, financial backing of the ASG was provided by Jamal Khalifa, a Saudi businessman who is reportedly the brother-in-law of Osama bin Laden. In 1998, Abdurajak was killed in a clash with Philippine police, and his brother Khadafi Janjalani assumed leadership. That said, the ASG is believed to be composed of many semiautonomous factions.

Similar to the MILF, the ASG seeks a separate Islamic state. However, given the scale and scope of terrorist acts committed, both the MNLF and the MILF have distanced themselves from the ASG. Moreover, the MNLF and MILF have denied any associations with other international terrorist organizations, including al Qaeda and Jemaah Islamiyah. Indeed, when a

New York Times article appeared in June 2003 that Mindanao had become the training center of Jemaah Islamiyah; representatives of the MILF and the Philippine government played down the allegations. Presidential spokesperson Ignacio Bunye said that the government was doing what it could to destroy terrorist cells in the southern Philippines. He explained, "We are not discounting that [*New York Times*] report. Everyone knows that terrorism is an international network now and these terrorist organizations could have established links not only in the Philippines, but also in other countries in Southeast Asia." MILF spokesperson Eid Kabalu likewise denied the report, adding that "they are fabricating linkages to pin us down as a terrorist group, but we are a legitimate revolutionary organization and we will survive this propaganda."[26]

THE COMMUNIST PARTY OF THE PHILIPPINES

Apart from Islamic separatist groups, a number of revolutionary movements have manifested in the Philippines. Indeed, historians write that, within Asia, "nationalism" first developed in the Philippines. This was associated with anti-Spanish movements, including the *ilustrados*—a reformist movement that included Jose Rizal—and the *Katipunan*. This later group, founded by Andres Bonifacio, advocated revolution and demanded the removal of the Spanish government. Another important movement, alluded to earlier, was the Hukbo ng Bayan Laban Hapon (People's Anti-Japanese Army). Established during World War II to resist Japanese occupying forces, the Huks eventually rebelled during the late 1940s and 1950s, when they were denied postwar representation and congressional seats in the newly independent Philippines. Socialist in orientation, the Huks were suppressed through U.S. covert activities.

The first Communist Party in the Philippines, the Partido Komunista Pilipinas (PKP) was founded in 1930. Jose Maria Sison, a member of the early PKP, split in the 1960s over personal and ideological differences in leadership. The PKP, in particular, was Soviet-influenced, whereas Sison favored a Maoist interpretation of communism. Officially formed in December 1968, the Communist Party of the Philippines (CPP) remains the most dominant insurgency in the Philippines. Sison was captured in 1976 during the Marcos martial law regime and subsequently spent nine years in solitary confinement. Upon his release, he was forced into exile and now lives in the Netherlands. Sison remains active, writing books and delivering speeches. He also serves as chief advisor to the National Democratic Front, the political wing of the CPP that was formed in 1976 by Father Luis Jalandoni in Utrecht, Netherlands. In 1995 Sison was granted political refugee status by the Dutch Supreme Court.

Supporting the CPP is its military wing, the New People's Army (NPA). Formed in March 1969, the NPA is likewise a Maoist-inspired guerrilla force committed to overthrowing the Philippine government. Sison ostensibly maintains control over activities, but, as discussed later, this is subject to question. Operationally, the NPA primarily targets local politicians, judges, government informers, as well as members of the Armed Forces of the Philippines (AFP). Geographically, they are most active throughout Luzon, the Visayas, and parts of Mindanao.

Throughout the 1990s, there were repeated, and often ineffective, attempts to broker a peace between the government and the CPP–NPA. Talks stalled, in part, because of continued assassinations of government officials by NPA members, as well as clashes with the AFP. Most recently, the CPP claims that their designation as a "foreign terrorist organization" by the United States has adversely affected negotiations for a peace settlement with the Philippine government. In August 2003, apparently with the support of the Philippine government, the U.S. State Department designated the CPP as a "foreign terrorist organization." According to Gregorio Rosal, spokesperson for the CPP, "the AFP's stubborn rejection of negotiations is because of its pea-minded objective of preventing NPA from debunking the terrorist tagging by the US-Arroyo regime." This is accurate—to a point. As a foreign terrorist organization, the AFP is not inclined to negotiation with the CPP. Moreover, as indicated by Colonel Preme Monta, spokesperson for the Northern Luzon Command of the NPA, actions undertaken by the rebel group only continue to merit them the "terrorist" tag. The NPA, indeed, has openly admitted to assassinations, bombings, and other acts of violence. In January 2003, just months after being designated a foreign terrorist organization, the NPA assassinated former CPP leader Romulo Kintanar while he ate lunch in Quezon City. Kintanar, arrested by the military in 1991 and given amnesty in 1996, was a government consultant. Claiming responsibility for the killing, Rosal explained that "this is part of the . . . NPA's determination to make accountable to revolutionary justice those guilty of the most serious crimes against the revolution and the people." Rosal further justified the assassination by saying, "It was absolutely correct to put an end to [his] rotten, criminal, counterrevolutionary and bloody record."[27]

The assassination of Kintanar also points to a question over the guidance of the CPP–NPA. In response to the assassination, for example, Sison had claimed that it was conducted under the auspices of the U.S. Central Intelligence Agency. Defense secretary Angelo Reyes, in an interview, said that if Sison knew something about the killing, "then he was lying. But if he has no knowledge about it, then it only proves that he has lost authority over the activities of his comrades here."[28]

According to officials of the Philippine government, the CPP–NPA maintains 107 guerrilla fronts nationwide. Throughout 2003, it was asserted, terrorist activities committed by the NPA increased substantially. More significant, though, are allegations that the NPA is working more closely with the MILF. In January 2004 it was announced that antitank weapons used by NPA guerrillas in a raid on a power plant in Batangas (southern Luzon) were obtained from the MILF. These weapons, interestingly, were believed to be leftovers from the Afghanistan War in 1995, in which several MILF fighters trained and participated.[29]

Although ideologically dissonant—indeed, as explained earlier, the MILF separated from the MNLF in part because of resistance to the Marxist ideology espoused by the latter group—the CPP and MILF have apparently forged an alliance in light of increased AFP military operations in the country. Defense secretary Eduaro Ermita explained that the two groups "go by the dictum that the enemy of my enemy is my friend." That enemy, according to Ermita, is the AFP. However, MILF spokesperson Eid Kabalu denounced this interpretation, saying only that the "alliance was forged merely to prevent our group and their group from clashes in areas where we both operate, particularly in Central Mindanao." He stated that the alliance does not include the sharing of weapons.[30]

PRESIDENT GLORIA MACAPAGAL-ARROYO

Born April 5, 1947, Gloria Macapagal-Arroyo is the daughter of former Philippine president Diosdado Macapagal and Eva Macaraeg Macapagal. After attending high school at the Assumption Convent (1960–1964), Macapagal-Arroyo received a bachelor's degree (1968) in commerce and economics from Assumption College. She later earned a master's degree (1978) in economics from Ateneo de Manila University and a doctorate (1985) in economics from the University of the Philippines. Her early career path was that of academia; she taught in various capacities at Ateneo de Manila University, Assumption College, and the University of the Philippines. During the presidential administration of Corazon Aquino, Macapagal-Arroyo served as assistant secretary in the Department of Trade and Industry (1987–1989) and later as undersecretary (1989–1992). She also served as executive director of the Garments and Textile Export Board.

In 1992, Macapagal-Arroyo ran for public office and was elected to the Senate. Three years later she was reelected to the Senate in 1995 with sixteen million votes—the highest number of votes received by any politician for any position in Philippine electoral history. Macapagal-Arroyo considered running for president in 1998 but, in the end, agreed to run for vice president. In the Philippines, the president and vice president are elected separately by direct popular vote.

Macapagal-Arroyo was elected vice president. However, opposition party member Joseph Estrada emerged victorious as president. Estrada, perhaps in an attempt to solidify his administration, offered Macapagal-Arroyo, in addition to her responsibilities as vice president, a position in his cabinet as secretary of social welfare and development.

The presidency of Estrada was plagued with charges of corruption. Ultimately, impeachment proceedings began. As the campaign to remove Estrada from office neared a peak, Macapagal-Arroyo was in an audience with the pope at the Vatican. Upon returning to the Philippines, she immediately resigned her cabinet post and began an "alternative national agenda" in preparation of Estrada's likely removal from office. At the time, although a number of religious groups supported Macapagal-Arroyo, she was also charged with political opportunism. Crucially, however, the Armed Forces of the Philippines largely supported Macapagal-Arroyo.

Macapagal-Arroyo assumed the presidency in January 2001. The ascension of Macapagal-Arroyo is often compared to the "People's Power" revolution in 1986. On that occasion, Corazon Aquino came to power following the peaceful removal of then-president Ferdinand Marcos, the former dictator who ruled for twenty-one years, nine of which were under martial law. A significant difference, however, lies in the fact that Macapagal-Arroyo replaced a democratically elected president, whereas Aquino replaced a dictator. Although her assumption of the presidency was unanimously supported by the Philippine Supreme Court, this did not prevent several thousand Estrada supporters from storming the presidential palace. Macapagal-Arroyo was compelled to declare a "state of rebellion."

The presidential administration of Macapagal-Arroyo was borne of political maneuvering and internal factions. It is not surprising, therefore, that Macapagal-Arroyo has pursued a policy of solidarity and reconciliation in an effort to reunite the Philippines. However, these objectives are also part and parcel of her Catholic upbringing. Indeed, Macapagal-Arroyo believes—much as U.S. President Bush—that she became president through God's will. Speaking at the twenty-first National Prayer Breakfast on August 16, 2001, Macapagal-Arroyo explained, "While I do not believe in fate, I believe in divine providence. And as leaders of society, we are placed where we are because of a reason, because of a plan, a divine plan for all of us. And each one of us must pray to discern what that plan is, then act according to our best light to comply with that plan." The president then said that "the key in manifesting God's plan in our lives lies in our ability through prayer to discern his divine wisdom and to apply it in our daily lives." It was this application that Macapagal-Arroyo attempted to integrate into her administration. Macapagal-Arroyo referred to 2 Chronicles 7:14, when the Lord said, "If my people, who are called by my name, will humble themselves and pray and seek my face and turn from their wicked ways, then I will hear from heaven and will forgive their sin and will heal their land." Macapagal-Arroyo explained that for her, "to humble ourselves" means "staying detached from the trappings and perks of power. It means, reaching out to those who still carry hatred or cynicism in their heart. It means, forgiving those who have done wrong rather than using my power to do vengeance upon them."[31]

Macapagal-Arroyo likewise discerned God's plan to her bid for presidency in 2004. On December 30, 2002, Macapagal-Arroyo announced that she would not run for president in the elections of 2004. She explained that "it is God who puts ideas in my heart" and that "in my attendance at Mass, it felt to me like He was telling me that He chose me to become president because He also knows that when He tells me not to run, then I would not run."[32] Her decision constituted a sacrifice. "If I don't make this sacrifice, what will happen to our country. . . . To prevent all of this, a sacrifice is needed. The first one who should make the sacrifice is the one who leads the country." In response, Bishop Socrates Villegas, spokesperson of Manila Archbishop Jaime Cardinal Sin, described the announcement as "heroic," adding that "this is what 'country first before self' means."[33]

During the summer and fall of 2003, however, Macapagal-Arroyo was repeatedly questioned about her intentions to run for the presidency in 2004. She was jeered for seeking divine guidance to make a decision. To her critics, Macapagal-Arroyo said, "[To] those who were asking why God does not talk to them, maybe they don't pray with discernment. [Discernment is] part of our religion." She concluded by saying that she always turns to her religious convictions whenever she has to make important decisions.[34]

In September, Macapagal-Arroyo met with Pope John Paul II at the Vatican. She explained that there would be "no politics" in her scheduled dialogue with the pope; however, she was praying over whether she would backtrack from her decision not to seek a fresh mandate.[35] On October 4, 2003, she announced that she would run for president in the upcoming elections. In her speech, she explained that she reached the decision through her own discernment. She explained, "In making this decision, I could have invoked the prodding of my [political] party, the clamor of the people, the support of many. These, you know, are true and already made known by the media. But I am not motivated to run because I was thrust, shoved, urged or pressed. Nakikita ko ang higit pang sakripisyo at gagampanan ko it [I see the need for a bigger sacrifice and I will perform it]."[36]

In Ephesians 1:18 it is written, "I pray that the God of our Lord Jesus Christ may give you a spirit of wisdom and revelation as you come to know Him, so that, with the eyes of your heart enlightened, you may know what is the hope to which He has called you." Macapagal-Arroyo was seeking guidance to her calling. Macapagal-Arroyo continued, "Some ask why I changed my mind. What matters more is that I changed my mind because there is a higher cause—to change society. To change society in a way that flourishes our future. It would have been easier to take the road to retirement. Taking up the call laid before me exacts more courage, more sacrifice, more obedience to God and our people."[37] Macapagal-Arroyo declared that she was responding to God's call, that it was her duty to lead her people. As will become clear, this position conforms readily with that of Bush's "mandate" to lead humanity to a world free of terrorism and, I suggest, is an important element in the overall Philippines' Will to War.

Unlike Bush's declaration of his mission, however, Macapagal-Arroyo's is more circumspect. She concluded her speech declaring, "I pray to God to grant me the grace to heal our divided land; the fortitude to unite our people; and the courage to be truly a president of reconciliation. A president of reform and reconciliation bringing peace and unity and the Lord's bounty to all our people under God's divine providence."[38] In this message, Macapagal-Arroyo is indicating that her path is clear; she has been shown by God where she should lead the people of the Philippines. She is unsure, however, if God will grant her the grace, fortitude, and courage to carry out His plans.

Macapagal-Arroyo brings a political fundamentalism to the Philippine's foreign policy. Indeed, Macapagal-Arroyo stated forthrightly that she would stress her government's adherence to Catholic dictums. Before her dialogue with the pope, Macapagal-Arroyo said, "I want to discuss how the policies of our government are in agreement with the teachings of the Catholic church."[39] These would be based on adherence to a strict reading of the Bible and the doctrines of the Catholic church. To this end, in her inaugural speech of 2001, she identified four core beliefs to which the government should focus:

1. "We must be bold in our national ambitions, so that our challenge must be that within this decade, we will win the fight against poverty."
2. "We must improve moral standards in government and society, in order to provide a strong foundation for good governance."
3. "We must change the character of our politics, in order to create fertile ground for true reforms. Our politics and patronage must give way to a new politics of party programs and process of dialogue with the people."
4. "Finally, I believe in leadership by example. We should promote traits such as work ethic and a dignified lifestyle, matching action to rhetoric, performing rather than grandstanding."[40]

These core beliefs translate, I suggest, into a political fundamentalism. Macapagal-Arroyo promoted a morally informed politics, one based on Catholic teachings. Significantly, her moral politics is also infused with a strong element of economic globalization. Not surprisingly, Macapagal-Arroyo's representation of globalization is theological: an underlying, unrelenting force that drives nations and their economies forward. She explained in her 2001 inaugural address that "the world of the 21st century that our youth will inherit is truly a new economy, where relentless forces such as capital market flows and advances in information and communications technology create both peril and opportunity." She continued, "To tap the opportunities, we need an economic philosophy of transparency and private enterprise, for these are the catalysts that nurture the entrepreneurial spirit to be globally competitive." She added that concurrently, however, "to address the perils, we must give a social bias to balance our economic development, and these are embodied in safety nets for sectors affected by globalization."[41] In short, Macapagal-Arroyo advocated a neoliberal position in her quest to eliminate poverty. This quest, though, must be morally informed. It has been this dualistic approach to foreign policy that accounts for the Philippines' deployment of foreign workers and the government's subsequent recall of its peacekeeping forces.

NOTES

1. Office of the President, "Remarks by President Gloria Macapagal-Arroyo at the State Arrival Ceremony," May 20, 2003, www.op.gov.ph/speeches (July 26, 2004).

2. Jim Garmone, "Coalition of the Willing Provides Formidable Force," American Forces Press Service, March 19, 2003, www.q77.com/iraqwar/afpnews/afp182.htm (August 22, 2004).

3. Garmone, "Coalition of the Willing."

4. Sarah Anderson, Phyllis Bennis, and John Cavanagh, "Coalition of the Willing or Coalition of the Coerced? How the Bush Administration Influences Allies in its War on Iraq," 2003, www.ips-dc.org (August 22, 2004).

5. David Domke, *God Willing? Political Fundamentalism in the White House, the "War on Terror," and the Echoing Press* (London: Pluto Press, 2004), 6–7.

6. James A. Tyner, *Made in the Philippines: Gendered Discourses and the Making of Migrants* (London: Routledge, 2004).

7. Paul Reuber, "The Tale of the Just War—a Poststructuralist Objection," *Arab World Geographer* 6 (2003): 44–46 (quote on 44).

8. Michel Foucault, *The Archaeology of Knowledge and the Discourse on Language,* trans. A. M. Sheridan Smith (London: Tavistock, 1972), 99.

9. Gordon L. Clark and Michael Dear, *State Apparatus: Structures and Language of Legitimacy* (Boston: Allen and Unwin, 1984), 87.

10. Murray Edelman, *Political Language: Words That Succeed and Policies That Fail* (New York: Academic Press, 1977), 142. See also Jenny Edkins, *Poststructuralism and International Relations: Bringing the Political Back In* (London: Lynne Rienner, 1999).

11. Eve K. Sedgwick, *Epistemology of the Closet* (Berkeley: University of California Press, 1990), 27.

12. Anderson, Bennis, and Cavanagh, "Coalition of the Willing."

13. Anderson, Bennis, and Cavanagh, "Coalition of the Willing."

14. Philip F. Kelly, *Landscapes of Globalization: Human Geographies of Economic Change in the Philippines* (London: Routledge, 2000), 26. See also Brian McAllister Linn, *The Philippine War, 1899–1902* (Lawrence: University of Kansas Press, 2000).

15. Stanley Karnow, *In Our Image: America's Empire in the Philippines* (New York: Random House, 1989), 10.

16. Richard E. Welch Jr., *Response to Imperialism: The United States and the Philippine-American War, 1899–1902* (Chapel Hill: University of North Carolina Press, 1979), 42.

17. Kelly, *Landscapes of Globalization,* 29.

18. Anthony Woodiwiss, *Globalisation, Human Rights, and Labour Law in Pacific Asia* (Cambridge: Cambridge University Press, 1998), 2, 102.

19. Woodiwiss, *Globalisation, Human Rights,* 102.

20. John Cooley, *Unholy Wars: Afghanistan, America, and International Terrorism* (London: Pluto Press, 2002), 182–83.

21. Abdelouahed Belkeziz, "Speech of H.E. Dr. Abdelouahed Belkeziz, the Secretary-General of the Organization of the Islamic Conference, at the Inauguration of the Tenth Session of the Islamic Summit Conference," Organization of Islamic Conference, www.oic-oci.org/press/english/october2003/sg10summit.htm (August 19, 2004).

22. Madge Kho, "A Conflict That Won't Go Away," www.philippineupdate.com/Conflict.htm (September 2, 2002).

23. Welch, *Response to Imperialism*, 40–41.

24. Thomas McKenna, *Muslim Rulers and Rebels: Everyday Politics and Armed Separatism in the Southern Philippines* (Berkeley: University of California Press, 1998).

25. David J. Steinberg, *The Philippines: A Singular and a Plural Place* (Boulder, Colo.: Westview Press, 1994), 126.

26. Ma. Theresa Torres, "Palace: Terror Cells Exist," *Manila Times*, June 2, 2003, www.manilatimes.net/national/2002/jun/02/top_stories20030602top1.html (March 31, 2004).

27. Joel San Juan, "NPA: We Killed Romy Kintanar," *Manila Times*, January 27, 2003, www.manilatimes.net/national/2003/jan/2/top_stories/20030127top1.html (August 4, 2004).

28. San Juan, "We Killed Romy."

29. Karl B. Kaufman and Ma. Theresa Torres, "NPA Raiders' Arms Came from MILF," *Manila Times*, January 14, 2004, www.manilatimes.net/national/2004/jan/14/yehey/top_stories/20040114top7.html (August 4, 2004).

30. Kaufman and Torres, "NPA Raiders."

31. Office of the President, "PGMA's Speech during the 21st National Prayer Breakfast," August 16, 2001, www.opnet.ops.gov.ph/speech-2001aug15.htm (August 23, 2004).

32. Stefan J. Bos, "Philippines President Arroyo Says God Told Her Not to Run in Next Election," *Bible Network News*, December 30, 2002, www.biblenetworknews.com/asiapacific/123002_philippines.html (August 9, 2004).

33. Bos, "God Told Her."

34. Efren L. Danao, "Cheers, Jeers Greet Arroyo's Announcement," *Manila Times*, October 5, 2003, www.manilatimes.net/national/2003/octo/05/top_stories/20031005top6.html (August 11, 2004); Maila Ager, "GMA Refuses to Bare 2004 Plans—Again," *Manila Times*, September 27, 2003, www.manilatimes.net/national/2003/sept/27/top_stories/2003092top4.html (August 11, 2004).

35. GMA News, "President to Stress Government Obedience to Catholic Church," September 26, 2003, www.inq7.net/brk/2003/sep/26/text/brkpol_6-1-p.htm (August 10, 2004).

36. Office of the President, "PGMA's Speech during the Pampanga Senior Citizens Congress and Formal Declaration to Run in the May 2004 Elections," October 4, 2003, www.op.gov.ph/speeches/ (August 11, 2004).

37. Office of the President, "Declaration to Run."

38. Office of the President, "Declaration to Run."

39. GMA News, "Government Obedience."

40. Office of the President, "PGMA's Inaugural Speech as the 14th President of the Republic of the Philippines," January 20, 2001, www.opnet.ops.gov.ph/speech-2001jan20.htm (August 9, 2004).

41. Office of the President, "Inaugural Speech."

2

THE POLITICS OF EMPLOYMENT

In all labor there is profit,
but the talk of the lips tends only to penury.

Proverbs 14:23

In 1995, a series of foreign crises transformed the Philippines' overseas employment program. The first centered on Flor Contemplacion, a female domestic worker employed in Singapore.[1] Contemplacion, in 1991, was charged with the double murder of another Filipina domestic worker—Delia Maga—and a four-year-old Singaporean boy. Contemplacion pleaded guilty to both charges and in 1995 was sentenced to death. Rumors circulated, however, that Contemplacion was innocent and had been pressured into a confession. Throughout the trial, Contemplacion was portrayed as a martyr, one of the many Filipinas who "sacrifice" their lives for the greed of the Philippine government. During the weeks leading up to the scheduled date of execution, Philippine president Fidel Ramos requested a stay of execution from the Singaporean government, and Catholic church leader Jamie Sin sought the intervention of Pope John II. These attempts went for naught, however, and on March 17, 1995, Contemplacion was executed.

The public response in the Philippines was immediate: public protests were held; the Singaporean flag was burned. Adding to the furor was the fact that on the day of the execution, Ramos was traveling throughout West Asia and Europe negotiating for trade and investment for the country; this increased public sentiment that the government was willingly sacrificing Contemplacion for monetary reasons. Criticism of the Philippine government was widespread, including the denouncing of the Philippine ambassador to Singapore and other various top-ranking officials of the Philippine

Overseas Employment Administration (POEA). As Juan L. Gonzalez concludes, "Contemplacion's death heightened long-standing debates in the Philippines and exposed the lack of adequate government attention to the plight of Filipino overseas contract workers, not just in Singapore, but in all the labour-receiving countries."[2]

Just months after the execution of Contemplacion, Sarah Balabagan went on trial for murder. Balabagan was a fifteen-year-old girl who entered the United Arab Emirates on a forged passport (she claimed to be twenty-eight years old to bypass POEA regulations). In July 1994, Balabagan was allegedly attacked and raped by her eighty-five-year-old male employer. Acting in self-defense, Balabagan overpowered the man and killed him. At the conclusion of the trial, Balabagan was found guilty of manslaughter and sentenced to seven years' imprisonment. Paradoxically, she was also awarded a settlement of US$27,000 for being raped.

Neither the prosecution nor the defense was satisfied with the ruling. Relatives of the employer insisted that seven years' imprisonment was inadequate punishment; Balabagan's lawyers countered that she was in fact innocent, that she acted in self-defense and thus should not be sent to prison. In September 1995, the prison sentence was indeed overruled, but Balabagan was instead, incredulously, resentenced—to death. Following the public outcry and political furor of the recent execution of Contemplacion, the potential execution of another Filipina domestic worker initiated substantial public protest in the Philippines and elsewhere around the world. Ultimately, the president of the United Arab Emirates intervened, and after a series of negotiations, relatives of the slain employer agreed to drop their demands for execution in return of a "blood" payment of approximately US$41,000. In October, Balabagan was sentenced a third time, this time receiving one hundred cane lashes and a twelve-month prison term (of which she served approximately eight months).

The events in 1995 contributed to the most significant reorganization—though not transformation—of the Philippines' overseas employment program since 1982 (detailed later in the chapter). In April 1995, following the execution of Contemplacion, the Department of Labor and Employment distributed a "White Paper on Overseas Employment." This document provided relevant information to the Philippine Congress as it was set to deliberate a series of bills drafted to protect migrant workers. As the summer-long drama of Balabagan dragged on, Ramos, on June 7, 1995, signed Republic Act (RA) 8042, an act that emerged from the consolidation of House Bill 14314 and Senate Bill 2077. Hailed as the Magna Carta of overseas employment, the Migrant Workers and Overseas Filipino Act of 1995, as RA 8042 was titled, signaled a sea change in the government's approach to overseas employment. Specifically, RA 8042 was an explicit avowal by the government that it did *not* promote overseas employment as part of the country's development program.

But despite the rhetoric, the Philippine state did support overseas employment and would continue to do so, retaining its place as the world's leader of government-sponsored contract labor migration. In 1995, approximately 650,000 migrant workers were deployed from the Philippines; by 1998 the number increased to over 750,000. In 2003, a total of 820,616 Filipinos left the country for overseas work; remittances from 2002 alone exceeded US$6 billion. Geographically, Filipinos lived and worked in over 194 destinations. Measured by sheer numbers or spatial extent, the Philippines continues to be the world's largest exporter of government-sponsored contract labor.

Overseas employment, in essence, supports the Philippines' economy. And this is an understanding of the Philippines' Will to War that must be situated within the context of transnational labor migration. As I argue in the course of this book, the administration of President Gloria Macapagal-Arroyo aggressively supported the United States' planned invasion of Iraq as well as the U.S.-led War on Terror. And overseas labor informed the decision of Macapagal-Arroyo to break her alliance with the United States, a decision that led to her dismissal from the Coalition of the Willing. If, in understanding the Middle East, as David Harvey writes, it's "all about oil," then in the Philippines, it's all about labor.[3]

Why this should be relates to the capital accumulation process associated with government-regulated transnational contract labor migration. Contemporary migration systems reflect an increasingly institutional basis in that many governments, especially those within the periphery, use labor-export programs as development strategies. This is seen, for example, in Sri Lanka, Pakistan, Indonesia, Bangladesh, and the Philippines. Governments attempt, through the export of labor, to reduce unemployment and unemployment levels, increase human capital as workers return with skills acquired abroad, and increase foreign revenues through the mandatory remittances of workers.

The Philippine government "employs" labor as an export commodity. Operationally, the Philippine government, through the POEA, seeks out optimal locations for worker deployment. In 2002, for example, the Philippine government participated in eight overseas missions to nine countries: Belgium, Germany, Hong Kong, Italy, Malaysia, the Netherlands, Saudi Arabia, the United Kingdom, and the United States. Although these missions may address working conditions and abuses of migrant rights, the underlying purpose is often to market Filipino workers to prospective governments and corporations.

The term *variable capital* refers to the sale, purchase, and use of labor power as a commodity. This is, as Harvey explains, a circular process.[4] The laborer (a person) sells labor power (a commodity) to the capitalist to use in the labor process in return for a money wage, which permits the laborer to purchase capitalist-produced commodities in order to live, in order to return to work, and so on. Within systems of overseas employment, however, the state is, in effect, in the position of selling labor power in return for foreign exchange. The significance of this is further illustrated with reference to Harvey's critique of classical location theory. It is commonly understood, for example, that the "spatial range of a good" is defined by the radial distance from a point of production where the market price places the good beyond what consumers are willing or able to pay for it. Thus, for instance, a consumer is more likely to travel a farther distance for a valuable commodity (a car) than for a loaf of bread. Harvey points out, though, that goods do not take themselves to market; merchants do. Spatially, this is what contributes to the continued expansion of capitalism as firms continue to search for alternative and better locations to sell their goods and services.

Overseas employment provides an interesting twist on the mobility of capital through the addition of human migration. On one hand, we can speak of the migration of capital to sites of labor. In this instance, capitalists may seek out locations where labor costs are lower or, alternatively, where labor is more disciplined (e.g., strikes and unions are banned). On the other hand, it is possible to speak of the migration of labor to sites of capital accumulation. Here, migrant workers literally embody the circulation of variable capital in that, through their remittances, the sending country is able to tap into locations of surplus capital. In the Philippines, migrant workers are *required* to remit a substantial portion of their earnings through Philippine financial channels. The amount varies by occupation but is usually on the order of 50 percent to 70 percent of the worker's salary. Consequently, through mandatory remittances, the Philippine state is able to use migrant workers as a form of mobile capital accumulation. This lies at the heart of critiques against the Philippines' commodification of migrant workers and provides the basis for accusations that the Philippine government sacrifices its people for profit. Such is the context for the Philippines' Will to War.

THE GENESIS OF THE PHILIPPINE MIGRATION INDUSTRY

Philip Kelly writes that "while the Philippines has long been integrated within the world economy, the nature of this relationship has shifted significantly in the last few decades." He further contends that "the historical experience of globalization in the Philippines cannot be understood in terms of exogenous forces bearing down upon a passive and pliable site." Thus, the emergence of the Philippines' overseas employment program must be viewed as a deliberate attempt by the Philippine state to readily incorporate itself into the changing global political economy.[5]

Government involvement in the export of labor actually dates to 1915 when the Philippine legislature passed Act 2486. Early efforts were minimal, however, and the initiation of an effective governmental regulation of overseas employment did not materialize until the martial law regime (1972–1981) of President Ferdinand Marcos. Marcos's "New Society" was framed as a means to rectify existent social, political, and economic problems that were plaguing the country. Economic policies were designed primarily to attract new private investment as Philippine development policy became increasingly oriented toward export production. Indeed, following the success of other Asian states (e.g., South Korea and Singapore), Marcos promised his version of "martial law, Philippine style."[6]

Before Marcos's time, the Philippine economy was structured around a strategy of import substitution that favored capital-intensive, large-scale industrialization. It became evident, however, by the late 1960s, that this approach was unable to meet the emerging needs of the economy. Many of the older, established manufacturing industries were unable to expand beyond the limited, protected home market, and industrial growth could not keep pace with the rapidly expanding population, estimated at seven hundred thousand annual entrants into the labor force. Moreover, various transformations of the world economy, including a decline in the value of Philippine exports and the growth in overseas borrowings, converged to hinder economic growth. In response, the Philippine government embarked on a dual economic strategy of export-oriented industrialization and its foreign counterpart, overseas employment.

Within a political environment of martial law, Marcos facilitated a major reorganization of labor relations within the country, changes that ultimately weakened the position of national labor. Marcos sought, ostensibly, to construct a New Society to rectify existing social, political, and economic problems confronting the country. Among these problems were the emerging communist insurgencies and Muslim separatist movements that continue to define the Philippines today. At the time, however, Marcos attempted to suppress these movements, as well as "legitimate" political oppositions, as he concentrated power within his circle of friends.

Marcos's New Society was predicated on an ideology that emphasized individual and national discipline and, concurrently, the sacrifice of personal liberties for economic development. From the outset, therefore, labor-related policies in the contemporary Philippines have sacrificed individual "bodies" for a more "global" vision of the nation-state. This is an observation that reappears in the context of Macapagal-Arroyo's decision regarding the kidnaping of Angelo de la Cruz—a point I return to in chapter 5. The New Society, however, was constructed on a repressive labor policy that banned strikes, eliminated unions, and entailed a downward revision of existing labor protection standards. The 1974 Labor Code, for example, as well as subsequent presidential decrees, favored foreign investors, selected members of the landed oligarchy, and Marcos personally. General Order 5, as a case in point, imposed a total ban on strikes and other forms of public assembly. This was later amended to limit the ban on strikes to only "vital" industries, which, not surprisingly, included companies engaged in the production or processing of essential commodities or products for export. The Labor Code, likewise, permitted employers to pay new employees only 75 percent of the basic minimum wage during a six-month probationary period. By releasing workers after this period, multinational corporations effectively instituted a high turnover rate, thereby reducing labor costs even more. Marcos claimed that the loss of civil liberties was a regrettable but temporary price that Filipinos would have to pay for political stability, economic growth, and social reform.[7]

As codified in the 1974 Labor Code, all labor policies and programs were to be realigned with overall development goals. Article 3 of the Labor Code specifies that the "state shall afford protection to labor, promote full employment, ensure equal work opportunities regardless of sex, race or creed, and regulate the relations between workers and employers." Additionally, as indicated in article 12, it is the policy of the state to (1) promote and maintain a state of full employment through manpower training, (2) protect every citizen desiring to work locally or overseas through the securing of the best possible terms and conditions of employment, (3) facilitate a free choice of available employment, and (4) facilitate and regulate the movement of workers in conformity with the national interest. Last, as mandated in articles 17.1 and 17.2, the Philippine state was to promote the overseas employment of Filipino workers through a comprehensive market promotion and development program and, in the process, secure the best possible terms and conditions of employment of Filipino contract workers on a government-to-government basis.[8]

The export of labor conformed with the Marcos regime's policy of development diplomacy, which was predicated on observation that "less-developed" countries contained large population bases as well as vital natural resources and that these could be used for development goals—hence, the use of the country's surplus labor and the high demand for labor, especially in oil-producing countries. Subsequently, the incipient Philippine "migration industry" capitalized on newly emerging employment opportunities throughout the Middle East and Asia. Before the oil embargo of 1973–1974, the Middle East labor market was characterized by a high degree of inter-Arab migration. In general, workers from oil-poor but labor-rich states (e.g., Yemen) supplied labor to other states. Moreover, the scale of industrialization was such that regional migration could well meet any labor demands. The oil embargo, however, changed the Gulf labor market. Increases in oil production, government royalties, and price combined to drive up revenues accruing to the oil-export states of the region by over 600 percent in constant dollars between 1972 and 1984. Consequently, with increased revenues, many Middle East states (e.g., Saudi Arabia, Kuwait, the United Arab Emirates, and Bahrain) initiated massive infrastructure projects.[9]

With the massive infusion of capital into the region, relative and absolute labor shortages ensued. Regional systems of migration could no longer match the needs of capital. In response, Gulf states began recruiting foreign workers from East Asia, South Asia, and Southeast Asia. South Korea was an earlier contributor, followed by other countries, including Pakistan, Sri Lanka, Thailand, and the Philippines. Local governments were quick to realize the advantages of hiring non-Arab migrant workers. Apart from providing a source of skills in volumes no longer available in the Gulf, migrant workers from Asia were generally confined to isolated work camps and would then depart when the project was finished. This was especially attractive to the smaller, less-populous states, such as the United Arab Emirates. And relatedly, there had been a growing uneasiness toward Arab migrants who would potentially decide to resettle after migration. This was not the case with Asian workers who, culturally estranged from the local populations, had no desire to stay and settle and who exerted almost no pressure to bring dependents.[10]

Overseas employment was (and continued to be) deemed beneficial as well to labor-exporting countries in Asia, including the Philippines. First, overseas employment is expected to reduce levels of unemployment and underemployment. In countries with high population-growth rates, this may be a significant benefit. Second, temporary migrant workers are presumed to improve the stock of human capital as workers return with skills acquired from abroad. Third, the export of labor is premised to promote development and alleviate the balance of payment problems through mandatory remittances. And herein lies the primary motivation behind the Philippines' continued support of overseas employment. As specified in article 22 of the 1974 Labor Code, all Filipino workers were required to remit a portion of their foreign earnings through Philippine financial channels. Consequently, between 1975 and 1994, Filipino overseas contract workers remitted approximately US$18 billion; this represented nearly 3 percent of the country's gross national product. Moreover, remittances have become a major component of the country's total export earnings. By 1992, for example, remittances as a proportion of overall exports goods and services reached a record high of 12.7 percent. And finally, in aggregate terms, the amount of earnings contributed to the gross national product by remittances from 1975 to 1994 (the aforementioned US$18 billion) was approximately four times larger than the total foreign direct investment for the same period.[11]

To take advantage of the rapidly changing global labor market, especially the opportunities in the Middle East, the Philippines required an efficient organizational structure. Consequently, the government reorganized the overseas employment program to consist of three subapparatuses: the newly created Overseas Employment Development Board and the National Seaman Board, and the existing Bureau of Employment Services. These were housed within the Ministry of Labor and Employment, which was later renamed the Department of Labor and Employment. The Overseas Employment Development Board and National Seaman Board were responsible for the promotion, marketing, and general regulation of land-based and sea-based workers, respectively. The Bureau of Employment Services was a government-run temporary employment agency. Consequent to the institutionalization of transnational migration, Philippine labor export increased by 53 percent between 1975 and 1976 and by 91 percent between 1976 and 1977.

Consistent with the increasingly centralized regime of Marcos, the form of the Philippines' overseas employment program was intended to be a government monopoly. This was similar to other areas of the economy, such as various agro-export sectors.[12] This was to be accomplished by the gradual phaseout of all private recruitment agencies. A government monopoly, however, failed to materialize for a number of reasons, not least of which was that the government discovered that it was in no position to adequately capitalize on the dynamic global labor markets and thus profit from the mandatory remittances of overseas workers. Additionally, coalitions of private recruitment agencies, such as the Philippine Association of Service Exporters, were established to better lobby for renewed participation. In 1978, the signing of Presidential Degree 1412 removed most restrictions on the activities of private labor recruiters. Subsequently, under the state–private sector partnership, the magnitude of overseas employment increased rapidly. Between 1975 and 1982, for example, the total number of processed workers increased by 772 percent.

The evolution of the Philippines' labor-export policy has also imparted a particular institutional form among nongovernment participants. Of special importance is the position assumed by Philippine construction companies. Within the Philippines, there are certain channels for the recruitment and deployment of workers. Specifically, these labor transfers may take place through name-hires (people hired through personal contacts rather than government or private agencies), private recruitment agencies, construction firms, or government placements. Historically, the recruitment of construction workers to supply foreign firms in the private sector is the domain of "construction companies" while "private recruiters" and the recruitment arm of the government engage all other land-based workers. As Charles Stahl explains, this division between construction companies and private recruitment agencies assumed special importance during the rush to secure Middle East contracts during the 1970s. At that time, it became apparent that employment prospects in the Middle East were going to greatly expand. Filipino construction companies convinced certain government officials that an uncontrolled flow of workers would prejudice the competitiveness of Philippine contractors. Accordingly, the government prohibited any firm other than a Filipino construction company from hiring Filipino construction workers (other occupations were not affected). The end result of this prohibition meant that Filipinos could work in the Middle East only as employees of a Filipino contractor. Furthermore, the method of supplying construction workers is based on subcontracting. Philippine construction companies approach foreign firms that have secured construction contracts and submit bids with regard to the supply price of different categories of labor. If they secure the subcontract, the Philippine construction company recruits and deploys workers to the principal contractor.[13]

The organizational structure of the Philippines' "migration industry" has changed over the years.[14] In 1982, a major change occurred when the Overseas Employment Development Board, the National Seaman Board, and the Bureau of Employment Services were merged to form the Philippine Overseas Employment Administration (POEA). This reorganization, as Maruja Asis writes, signaled an intensified effort on behalf of the Philippine government to capitalize on the global economy and use overseas employment as a national development strategy.[15] As codified in Presidential Decree 797, the POEA was tasked with the formulation, implementation, and monitoring of overseas employment; in short, it assumed a largely regulatory function. Operationally, the POEA concentrated mostly on the regulation of private recruitments—of which there are approximately two thousand licensed agencies in the Philippines—and the marketing of workers. The private sector would be largely responsible for the actual recruitment and placement of overseas workers.

The policies and subsequent practices of the POEA suggest that overseas employment as forwarded in the Philippines is not seen as part of the mainstream national economy. Rather, overseas employment is portrayed as a means unto itself. This approach to overseas employment remained in effect following the ascension of Corazon Aquino as president. Under the Aquino administration, the government responsibility toward overseas employment remained focused primarily on the marketing of workers and secondarily on the welfare of workers. As specified in the *Rules and Regulations Governing Overseas Employment*, it is the policy of the POEA to promote and develop overseas employment opportunities in cooperation with relevant government institutions and the private sector; establish a conducive environment for the continued operation of legitimate, responsible, and professional private recruitment agencies; provide protection to Filipino workers and their families; and develop and implement programs for the effective monitoring, retraining, and reemployment of returning contract workers. The philosophy of the overseas employment program is detailed in the inaugural issue of the *Overseas Info Series* (an in-house journal published by the marketing branch of the Preemployment Services Division of the POEA):

> A discriminate marketing approach guides the development of labor markets for Filipino overseas contract workers. Tapping non-traditional markets, whether skill-based or geographic-based, is geared towards high-benefit, high-growth areas suited for grooming a premium international image for the Filipino workers. Responding to future higher skills demand, it is the mission of our marketing program to equip itself with suitable surplus labor to fill demand trends. It is our further concern to ensure that no one market spoils our overall market image and/or blocks our entry to newly emerging opportunities. When net re-

turns are ascertained to be unfavorable in any market segment, it becomes our task to recommend suspension and/or closure of such market and pour resources into better alternatives. It is the program's responsibility to protect the well-being of the Filipino worker.[16]

Although the final sentence makes passing reference to the "well-being" of migrant workers, the overall thrust is one of market demand. The Philippine government, through the activities of the POEA, sought to fully incorporate itself into the labor markets of foreign areas. Significant also is the perceived necessity to diversify labor markets. On one hand, as indicated in the quotation, the POEA was concerned that an overemphasis in one area—such as the deployment of a certain occupation (e.g., domestic workers)—would skew the overall image of migrant Filipino labor. Thus, foreign institutions in the market for, say computer engineers, may not readily think of the Philippines as an option. On the other hand, the POEA's attempt to diversify markets is also related to foreign affairs. Especially following the 1991 Gulf War, the economic benefits of narrow geographic distributions of migrant workers were threatened by military conflicts. Thus, as an economic safeguard, efforts were made to increase the geographic dispersal of migrant workers. Last, this statement suggests that the primary concern of the POEA was not to utilize existing unemployed or underemployed labor—which was one of the perceived benefits—but instead to generate further surpluses of labor. This was to be accomplished through the enticement of Philippine citizens to participate more actively in overseas employment, as well as through the continued emphasis of job-training programs for (foreign-based) marketable occupations.

The presidential administration of Ramos (1992–1998) initially continued these practices. Under the National Economic Development Authority's Medium-Term Development Plan for 1993–1998, the Ramos administration's position was strong in stating that it would maximize the economic benefits, but it was weak on voicing its determination to minimize the social costs. Specifically, the plan announced that the country will

> continue the overseas employment program as an alternative source of employment opportunities, provided that this does not result in an undue drain in scientific/technical expertise and locally needed and middle-level skills. The program should be strengthened through adequate strategies to ensure the dignity and welfare of workers and their families.[17]

Ramos did suggest that as more industries located in the Philippines—thereby generating more domestic-based employment opportunities—the export of labor may gradually diminish in importance. Foreign crises, however, would radically alter the direction of the Philippines overseas employment. Following the events of 1995, the Philippine government ushered in the most significant overhaul of its overseas employment program since its inception in 1974. RA 8042, the "Magna Carta of overseas employment," was *not* an act designed to eliminate the export of labor; it was, however, a clarion call to reposition the government's responsibilities. As articulated in RA 8042:

> While recognizing the significant contribution of Filipino migrant workers to the national economy through their foreign exchange remittances, the State *does not promote overseas employment as a means to sustain economic growth and achieve national development.* The existence of the overseas employment program rests solely on the assurance that *the dignity and fundamental human rights and freedoms of the Filipino citizen shall not, at any time, be compromised or violated.* The State, therefore, shall continuously create local employment opportunities and promote the equitable distribution of wealth and the benefits of development.[18] (Italics added.)

RA 8042 is an explicit avowal by the government that it would not use overseas employment as part of the country's development strategy.[19] Additionally, in its promotion of human rights and freedoms for individual workers, RA 8042 constituted a neoliberal attack on the government regulation of overseas employment. Founded on the belief that people should be allowed maximum "freedom" to pursue their private projects, neoliberalism premises that states should play a minimal role in the day-to-day workers of markets. Indeed, proponents of neoliberalism declare that "free" markets, including labor markets, should be the keystone of development strategies.

In effect, RA 8042 was a means to reduce government intervention and, arguably, government culpability. Section 29 of RA 8042 mandated the Department of Labor and Employment to formulate a five-year comprehensive deregulation plan on recruitment activities; section 30 mandated a gradual phaseout of all regulatory functions occur within five years. As detailed by Rochelle Ball and Nicola Piper, the passage of this act was based on a strong endorsement of deregulating the responsibility of governmental institutions, supposedly in the name of worker welfare.[20] Consequently, the POEA responded with its own white paper on overseas employment. Entitled *Managing International Labor Migration and the Framework for the Deregulation of the POEA*, this paper was written to "allay fears about POEA deregulation and clarify deep seated concerns on [the POEA's] new paradigm of managing migration."[21]

As articulated in the white paper, the POEA under deregulation was to assume a new philosophy of overseas employment. The white paper contends, "Managing a global phenomenon starts with understanding the philosophy of humankind, dynamics of migration, history and natural laws which cannot be repealed." The POEA and other constituent parts of the Philippine state are thus portrayed as being "controlled" by the natural laws of globalization. The document continues that the "economic law of supply and demand is an irrepressible force in the global labor market," more so "now with the globalization era." Moreover, "this reality seems overshadowed by the application of national labour laws and administrative systems that perpetuate a pathological fallacy that labour migration is a program creation or innovation of government to address employment gaps."[22] In effect, the POEA has discursively constructed overseas employment as a natural feature of globalization; accordingly, people will seek employment opportunities to best meet their individual needs.

The white paper likewise positions the Philippines within the global economy: "Media sensationalism tends to overshadow the fact that the global presence of Filipino labour is our strategic contribution to the global development, from which we reap net rewards central to the goals of our social economy. Managing means being able to objectively recognize and subsequently dominate our niche and comparative advantage and empowering from our weakness."[23] This statement illuminates two key points. First, not only is transnational labor migration represented as an inherent feature of the global economy, but the Philippines has also been relegated by some natural law to a labor supply niche. Just as other countries are "blessed" with abundant supplies of natural resources such as oil, the Philippines has been blessed—according to the POEA—with abundant supplies of labor. Structural conditions—such as the promotion of export-oriented industrialization, the expansion of agribusiness, and inequitable distributions of land-ownership—fade dimly into the background. The Philippine state must, for the benefit of the country, capitalize on this market niche; this is to be accomplished not by the active promotion of migration but rather through the creation of a favorable market environment. As expressed in the white paper, "As human rights with democratic ideology, our migrant workers assert their constitutional rights and exercise their faculty of judgement to satisfy their socioeconomic needs and wants. No amount of legislative or other structural barriers can effectively suppress these natural drives and human rights unless enforcement of such barriers is undertaken strictly under an authoritarian regime."[24]

Apart from forwarding a neoliberal explanation of transnational labor migration, the POEA makes effective use, discursively, of the dictatorial regime of Marcos. Thus, in an ironic twist of historical interpretation, to deny Filipinos the right to seek overseas employment is equated with the very same authoritarian regime that contributed to the emergence of large-scale, government-sponsored overseas employment. The POEA has, consequently, constructed migrant workers as empowered individuals who express their constitutional and basic human rights of spatial movement. This forwarding of empowerment is captured in the concept of "full disclosure," as expressed in an earlier POEA position paper. Full disclosure "calls for the policy norm that: honesty is the best policy. To promote a culture of well-informed public is to stimulate a universal environment conducive to it." Moreover, full disclosure "is not a matter of recognizing and accepting one provision of the employment contract and rejecting the others. It is laying the cards on the table and when one makes a decision, he is primarily responsible for that decision."[25]

Through a neoliberal policy of full disclosure, all government and private institutions are tasked to provide all information—wages, working conditions, and so on—to empower potential workers to make informed decisions regarding overseas employment. The POEA thus seeks to empower individuals to make free and rational employment choices. However, the POEA further identifies that migrant empowerment will still require the verification of information. Hence, regulatory intervention is necessary and mandatory to ensure a proper functioning of the global labor market. Consequently, the POEA maintains a prerogative to maintain and impose standards, but the ultimate decision is that reached by the employer and employee, each with "full" understanding of the costs and benefits. Following the logic of this policy, of course, abused women and men are therefore considered to be willing participants in overseas migration through free and rational choice, with accountability for cases of exploitation being transferred to the migrants. Therefore, rather than increase worker welfare, the neoliberal transformation of the Philippines' overseas employment program actually undermined worker welfare through a state retreat from its responsibilities, with the transference of responsibility for exploitation away from government and private institutions and toward the migrants.[26]

The emergence of an "empowered migrant worker" has occurred simultaneously with other efforts of the Philippine state. As Kelly identifies, the Ramos administration elided the prescriptions of neoliberalism with the cause of personal freedom. The decision to migrate was seen as a liberating, empowering decision—a personal choice made in the context of the full understanding of the risks and rewards. As explained in the Medium Term Development Plan of 1995:

> The efforts of communicating the [Medium Term Development Plan]/ Philippines 2000 have been pushed into a more personal but dynamic dimension through the conceptualization of a modern Filipino role model—Juan Kaunlaran [John Progress]. As conceived, Juan Kaunlaran is the modern Filipino, empowered and globally competitive, who has risen above the self-deprecating images of the indolent Juan Tamad [John Lazy].[27]

As reinterpreted by the POEA, "Juan Kaunlaran" becomes an empowered, globally competitive migrant worker. Publically, the POEA's website affirmed this position in its statement that

> the Overseas Filipino Worker is the heart of our existence. He is competitive and employed productively. He continues to hone his skills through education and training. He contributes to the country's economic, social and cultural development through technology application in local industries and sharing of international experiences. . . . Recognizing that labour migration is a global phenomenon, we maintain overseas employment as one option for the fulfillment of his aspirations.[28]

The government, subsequently, promoted itself as an organization committed to the protection of individual rights, liberties, and freedoms. This countered the criticism, accordingly, that the state promotes or "exports" its workers in a quest for capital accumulation. Consequently, the state effectively upheld the democratic principles of free choice and the freedom of movement.

MORALITY, MIGRATION, AND NEOLIBERALISM

Since her inception as president in 2001, Macapagal-Arroyo has rearticulated the philosophies of the POEA and the overall export of labor. She has retained the neoliberal philosophies of full disclosure, transparency, and migrant empowerment. However, the Macapagal-Arroyo administration is also determined to utilize overseas employment as a means to sustain economic growth and achieve national development. Abandoning earlier discourses of "managed migration" and of migration being a natural process, the current administration is committed to an intensified program of worker deployment. Indeed, Macapagal-Arroyo has consistently set as a target the number of one million workers to be deployed in a single year. Likewise, she has promoted a philosophy based on increased efficiency and the removal of bureaucratic red tape. She has been forthright in her assertion that "Filipinos overseas will continue to play a critical role in the country's economic and social stability."[29]

In part, the Philippine president views the export of transnational labor as a vital part in the country's overall antipoverty efforts. During a 2001 speech delivered at the Second Annual Philippine Business Outlook Conference, for example, Macapagal-Arroyo affirmed her commitment to fighting poverty. She explained, "Our objective is to win the battle against poverty . . . and in order to accomplish this, we will pursue a disciplined program for economic growth that will entail encouraging free enterprise through an environment of transparency and a level playing field." Such an understanding is consistent with the education of the president. As she explained, "As an economist myself, I understand that without a credible policy framework and stability and without good governance, transparency and a level playing field, there is little that can be done to bring progress to our people." Macapagal-Arroyo identified the preferred course of action: "Our basic strategy is to rely on market forces to push economic growth." Accordingly, Macapagal-Arroyo's administration would intervene as little as possible, preferring instead to "let the private sector be the main driving force of the economy." In this way, the approach adopted by Macapagal-Arroyo conforms more readily with the earlier strategies of the POEA to relinquish the bulk of recruitment and deployment activities to the private sector. The Philippine state would provide an operating environment conducive to the requirements of private labor recruiters. Consequently, agencies such as the Department of Foreign Affairs and the POEA would concentrate on the securing of bilateral agreements and other multinational arrangements that impinge on foreign labor markets. This arrangement is made clear in Macapagal-Arroyo's statement: "We will reduce government intervention and competition from the marketplace."[30]

Macapagal-Arroyo's neoliberal approach to economic growth is also rooted firmly in her religious beliefs. In particular (and as discussed in more detail in chapter 4), Macapagal-Arroyo has incorporated a moral interpretation into her policy pronouncements. As explained during a 2001 meeting with the Foundation for Economic Freedom, Macapagal-Arroyo began by noting that the country "should try to build an economy that matches global benchmarks for efficiency and productivity." Therefore, specific steps must be taken, including the reduction of the budget deficit, the upgrading of labor skills through education and training programs, and a reformation of the tax system. However, Macapagal-Arroyo also explained that "it is clear that market forces, while they solve many problems, . . . do not solve every problem that communities confront." Economic growth could only be accomplished in an environment of competition, efficiency, hard work, and entrepreneurship. But underscoring this environment is, according to Macapagal-Arroyo, "good governance." By this, she explained that "good governance is about moral ascendancy." The government should thus be free of bribery and corruption. Moreover, "the task of improving moral standards in governance must be accompanied by constant improvement in the systems of government. Mechanisms of accountability need to be improved."[31]

A morally informed neoliberal philosophy is expressed in the *Medium-Term Philippine Development Plan, 2001–2004*, which affirms that "overseas employment remains to be a legitimate option for the country's work force. As such the government shall fully respect labor mobility, including the preference of workers for overseas employment. Protection shall be provided to Filipinos who choose to work abroad and programs to effectively reintegrate them into the domestic economy upon their return shall be put up. *Better employment opportunities and modes of engagement in overseas labor markets shall be actively explored and developed, consistent with regional and international commitments and agreements*."[32] This last statement is crucial, for it relates directly to the Philippines' Will to War.

During the Macapagal-Arroyo presidency, the government has aggressively pursued overseas employment as an economic tool. The POEA, specifically, has adopted a three-pronged strategy to actuate its production of overseas employment. One component is to sustain existing markets. Thus, the POEA works to ensure that it continues to deploy contract workers to its traditional markets, such as Singapore and Saudi Arabia. A second strategy is to expand existing markets. Japan provides a good example of this strategy. Currently, the majority of Philippine contract workers destined to Japan are employed as "entertainers" or "performing artists" (both generally taken to be euphemisms for "sex workers"). Under its new mandate, the POEA is attempting to diversify the Japanese market through the deployment of other types of workers, notably nurses and health care workers. Finally, the third strategy proposed by the POEA is to enter nontraditional labor markets or markets that have been closed in recent years. The countries of Germany, Ireland, and the United Kingdom, for example, have been targeted by the POEA as sites of potential deployment. And the POEA has indeed made appreciable gains in Europe. Whereas in 1998 only 502 Filipinos were deployed to England, over 10,500 workers were deployed in the first eight months of 2002; deployment to Ireland likewise increased, from only 18 to 3,260 in this same period. Overall, total deployment to Europe increased from 26,422 in 1998 to more than 43,000 in 2001.[33]

There is another angle to the Philippines' search for nontraditional markets, one that I term *anticipatory reactivism*. Policymaking in the Philippines has been largely reactionary when it comes to overseas employment. Maruja Asis attributes this to two factors. First, governmental management is of recent vintage; as such, its initial policies were fashioned without the benefits of historical precedents or a well-developed database. Second, the Philippines' overseas employment program was not envisioned to last so long. Indeed, the original planners of the government program believed that overseas labor migration would be a stopgap measure, one that could take advantage of the emerging opportunities in the Middle East following the oil embargo. In short, the approach to policymaking was reactive: policies were modified, or new ones were made as new challenges surfaced.[34]

Three decades later, the POEA has learned from past experiences. The POEA, in effect, is in a position to anticipate problems before they arise and, consequently, capitalize on events that may otherwise generate crises. In other words, the POEA is able to develop contingency plans to be utilized in case a particular "market" opens up. These openings may be associated with major infrastructure projects initiated by economic restructuring—such as when Taiwan opened its economy to foreign labor—or, as Iraq illustrates, military conflict.

The Philippines' Will to War signifies in part an attempt by the Philippine government to capitalize on the anticipated reconstruction projects that would arise following combat operations in Iraq. To take part in the reconstruction efforts in Iraq, the Philippine government needed to be seen as a staunch ally in the Coalition of the Willing. And clearly the Philippines' approach to overseas employment—with its neoliberal foundation—conformed readily with the Bush administration's promotion of freedom, liberty, and democracy, all under the aegis of the War on Terror. However, this explanation in and of itself is insufficient. Instead, as I argue in the remainder of this book, Macapagal-Arroyo viewed the coalition as a means to another end. In the Philippines, overseas employment is foreign policy; this association, however, is far from straightforward.

NOTES

1. For an extensive discussion of this incident, see R. J. May, "The Domestic in Foreign Policy: The Flor Contemplacion Case and Philippine-Singapore Relations," *Pilipinas* 29 (1997): 63–76.

2. Juan L. Gonzalez, *Philippine Labour Migration: Critical Dimensions of Public Policy* (Singapore: Institute of Southeast Asian Studies, 1998), 6.

3. David Harvey, *The New Imperialism* (Oxford: Oxford University Press, 2003).

4. David Harvey, *Spaces of Hope* (Berkeley: University of California Press, 2000), 101–16.

5. Philip F. Kelly, *Landscapes of Globalization: Human Geographies of Economic Change in the Philippines* (London: Routledge, 2000), 16; see also James A. Tyner, *Made in the Philippines: Gendered Discourses and the Making of Migrants* (London: Routledge, 2004).

6. Kelly, *Landscapes of Globalization*, 33; see also Walden Bello, D. Kinley, and E. Elinson, *Development Debacle: The World Bank in the Philippines* (San Francisco: Institute for Food and Development Policy, 1982); Gary Hawes, *The Philippine State and the Marcos Regime: The Politics of Export* (Ithaca, N.Y.: Cornell University Press, 1987); and W. H. Overholt, "Pressures and Policies: Prospects for Cory Aquino's Philippines," in *Rebuilding a Nation: Philippine Challenges and American Policy*, ed. Carl H. Lande (Washington, D.C.: Washington Institute Press, 1987), 89–110.

7. For further discussions, see S. Kuruvilla, "Economic Development Strategies, Industrial Relations Policies and Workplace IR/HR Practices in Southeast Asia," in *The Comparative Political Economy of Industrial Relations*, ed. K. Wever and L. Turner (Madison: Industrial Relations Research Association Series, University of Wisconsin, 1995), 115–50; David G. Timberman, *A Changeless Land: Continuity and Change in Philippine Politics* (New York: M. E. Sharpe, 1991); and E. M. Villegas, *The Political Economy of Philippine Labor Laws* (Quezon City, Philippines: Foundation for Nationalist Studies, 1988).

8. J. N. Nolledo, ed., *The Labor Code of the Philippines, with Implementing Regulations, Related Laws, and Other Issuances* (Manila: National Bookstore, 1993).

9. Peter N. Woodward, *Oil and Labor in the Middle East: Saudi Arabia and the Oil Boom* (New York: Praeger, 1988), 8.

10. Woodward, *Oil and Labor*, 9–10.

11. Gonzalez, *Philippine Labour Migration*, 73–75.

12. Hawes, *Politics of Export*.

13. Charles W. Stahl, *International Labor Migration: A Study of the ASEAN Countries* (New York: Center for Migration Studies, 1986), 6.

14. James A. Tyner, "The Spatial Structure of the Philippines' Overseas Employment Program," *Asian Geographer* 19 (2000): 139–56.

15. Maruja M. B. Asis, "The Overseas Employment Program Policy," in *Philippine Labour Migration: Impact and Policy*, ed. G. Battistella and A. Paganoni (Quezon City, Philippines: Scalabrini Migration Center, 1992), 68–112.

16. Philippine Overseas Employment Administration, "Market Development: Seeking Purpose and Promise for Filipino Skills," *Overseas Employment Info Series* 1 (1988): 5–9.

17. Gonzalez, *Philippine Labour Migration*, 124.

18. Philippine Overseas Employment Administration, *Migrant Workers and Overseas Filipinos Act of 1995: Republic Act 8042 and its Implementing Rules and Regulations* (Manila: Department of Labor and Employment, 1996), 2.

19. Gonzalez, *Philippine Labour Migration*, 128.

20. Rochelle Ball and Nicola Piper, "Globalisation and Regulation of Citizenship—Filipino Migrant Workers in Japan," *Political Geography* 21 (2002): 1013–34.

21. Richard R. Casco, *Managing International Labour Migration and the Framework for the Deregulation of the POEA* (Manila: Philippine Overseas Employment Administration, 1997), 2.

22. Casco, *Managing International Labour Migration*, 2–3.

23. Casco, *Managing International Labour Migration*, 4.

24. Casco, *Managing International Labour Migration*, 4; see also Tyner, *Made in the Philippines*, 46–47.

25. Richard R. Casco, *Full Disclosure Policy: A Philosophical Orientation* (Manila: Philippine Overseas Employment Administration, 1995), 4.

26. Tyner, *Made in the Philippines*, 48; see also Ball and Piper, "Globalisation and Regulation."

27. Quoted in Philip F. Kelly, "Globalization, Power, and the Politics of Scale in the Philippines," *Geoforum* 28 (1997): 151–71 (quote on 157).

28. James A. Tyner, "Migrant Labour and the Politics of Scale: Gendering the Philippine State," *Asia Pacific Viewpoint* 41 (2000): 131–54.

29. Office of the President, "PGMA's Speech during the Department of Foreign Affairs Foundation Day 2004," July 23, 2004, www.op.gov.ph/speeches (August 20, 2004).

30. Office of the President, "PGMA's Speech During the 2nd Annual Philippine Business Outlook Conference," March 1, 2001, www.opnet.ops.gov.ph/speech-2001 mar01a.htm (August 18, 2004).

31. Office of the President, "PGMA's Speech during the Meeting with the Foundation for Economic Freedom, Inc.," February 15, 2001, www.opnet.ops.gov .ph/speech-2001feb15.htm (August 18, 2004).

32. National Economic Development Authority, *The Medium-Term Philippine Development Plan, 2001–2004, with the 2001 State of the Nation Address* (Manila: National Economic Development Authority, 2001), 33.

33. Tyner, *Made in the Philippines*, 71–72.

34. Asis, "Overseas Employment Program," 69.

3

CONSTRUCTING WAR:
AMERICA'S WILL

*For it is God who works in you to will
and to act according to His good purpose.*

Philippians 2:13

On the evening of September 11, 2001, as the drama of the terrorist attacks continued to unfold, President Bush addressed the American
public. In his brief remarks, Bush set an agenda for the course of the nation.
He began by explaining, "Our fellow citizens, our way of life, our very freedom came under attack in a series of deliberate and deadly terrorist acts."
Bush was adamant that the attacks were *not* in response to any actions undertaken by the United States; he ruled out the possibility of American foreign policy or military presence as a possible motive. Rather, the acts committed against the United States, according to Bush, were motivated out of
cultural difference, irrational jealousies, and ultimately, the fact that evil ex-
ists in the world. Bush emphatically declared, "America was targeted for attack because we're the brightest beacon for freedom and opportunity in the
world." The statement, of course, ignored America's global political role in
the Middle East specially and the world more generally.[1]

In so arguing, Bush neutralized political discourse. He specified the
causes of the attack and the appropriate course of action. As David Domke
explains, "Instead of opening up the discourse and allowing a democratic
dialogue to take place, Bush's rhetoric hijacked the discussion about the
significance and implications of September 11, thereby denying to U.S. citizens important opportunities for national self-examination and a wide
public hearing of diverse viewpoints—and also shutting out the world,
must of which was extending unprecedented sympathy for U.S. citizens

and the nation."[2] The post–Cold War era would not be free from threats; instead, the world remained mired in a monumental struggle of good versus evil. Such was the geopolitical and geomoral vision forwarded by Bush. He explained, "Today, our nation saw evil, the very worst of human nature."[3] This vision would result in the military invasions of Afghanistan and Iraq. Regarding these statements and the subsequent military decisions, Peter Singer concludes that Bush's plan of action "was the most aggressive choice among a range of options that had not been adequately explored. It was an option chosen by a leader who was in a hurry to act, to show the American public that he was a leader, and to make an example of Afghanistan, in order to send a signal to other nations."[4]

Through his deliverance, Bush assumed the persona of a prophet, one ready and able to lead his people out of harm's way. Intoning his listeners— in the United States and beyond—to stand by him, Bush said, "America and our friends and allies join with all those who want peace and security in the world, and we stand together to win the war against terrorism. . . . And I pray they will be comforted by a power greater than any of us, spoken through the ages in Psalm 23: 'Even though I walk through the valley of the shadow of death, I fear no evil, for You are with me.'" With God on his side, Bush declared that a new war was confronting the United States. As subsequent speeches would clarify, this would not be the same type of war as previous wars. Instead, this war would be fluid, contingent, without borders— in short, it would be deterritorialized. And it was captured in the phrase "War on Terror."

Bush drew on other scriptures in his address. Invoking Matthew 12:30, in which Jesus declared, "He that is not with me is against me, and he that gathers not with me scatters abroad." Bush warned the world, "The search is underway for those who are behind these evil acts. . . . We will make no distinction between the terrorists who committed these acts and those who harbor them." Bush would reaffirm this message nine days later when he announced that America "will pursue nations that provide aid or safe haven to terrorism. Every nation, in every region, now has a decision to make. Either you are with us, or you are with the terrorists. From this day forward, any nation that continues to harbor or support terrorism will be regarded by the United States as a hostile regime."[5]

That the attacks of September 11, 2001, precipitated a crisis of horrific proportion is unarguable. This does mean, though, that the destruction wrought by terrorists was also used as a political resource to serve other agendas. Scholars of political language have noted that *crisis* is perhaps the most powerful political term available to garner public support. Murray

Edelman explains that "the word 'crisis' connotes a threat or emergency people must face together" and, furthermore, that "the language conventionally used to describe a crisis helps people to adapt to it by evoking a problematic picture of the issue."[6]

In the aftermath of September 11, the Bush administration put forward a particular narrative, but it is imperative to recognize that it was just one possible reading. French theorist Michel Foucault asserted that, in politics, there is a battle for "truth." For Foucault, however, "truth" does not refer to the ensemble of truth that is to be discovered and accepted but rather to the ensemble of rules according to which the true and false are separated. It is not, therefore, a battle "on behalf" of truth but instead a battle about what is accepted and circulated—what is "willed" as truth and how this understanding coincides with political and economic relations.[7]

The "will to truth" forms part of what Foucault termed a *political economy* of truth. In elaboration, Foucault specified some key conditions of how "truth" is willed. First, truth is embedded in particular discourses and the institutions that produce them (an ironic statement given the presence of "embedded" reporters in the invasion of Iraq). In other words, what is presented as truth is defined by those individuals and institutions that make use of "truthful" statements. Truth, moreover, is contingent on political, social, and economic demands. Truth is thus constructed to satisfy particular demands, such as to conform with today's consumer-oriented, sound-bite driven tendencies. Last, truth is mobile; it is produced, circulated, and consumed but also under the control—dominant, if not exclusive—of a few select political and economic apparatuses.[8]

My principle focus is on the Philippines' Will to War. However, it is not possible to fully comprehend the Philippines' foreign policy decisions regarding Iraq and the War on Terror without discussing America's Will to War. The jeremiad rhetoric of Bush in particular provided the pretext for the Coalition of the Willing. Through his public articulation of the new world order, foreign governments were impelled to take sides. Consequently, these governments would likewise publicly articulate *their* motivations and intentions to join or not to join the coalition. First, however, some background information on U.S.–Iraq relations is warranted.

LAYING THE FOUNDATION

All states are constructed, many through violent acts. The Republic of Iraq was borne of colonial aggressions. Following World War I, the victorious

British and French governments agreed to divide up the former territory of the Turkish-controlled Ottoman Empire. France gained control of what would become present-day Syria and Lebanon; Britain assumed control over Palestine and Iraq. In 1921, the Kingdom of Iraq was formally established, with Emir Faisal ibn Hussain as King.

During the 1920s, Western powers, including Britain, the United States, France, and the Netherlands, increased their activities in the region. Oil exploration in particular was pursued, largely under the auspices of the colonial-controlled Iraqi Petroleum Company. Although Iraq gained its political independence in 1932, the country remained bound within a neocolonial relationship, its economy dominated by the petroleum company.

Following World War II, the Middle East continued to be viewed as a vital strategic location. Accordingly, both Western and Soviet politicians interfered in the state-building processes of the region. Within Iraq specifically, the pro-British constitutional monarchy of Iraq was overthrown in a military coup in 1958. The action brought Abdul Karim Kassem to power. In response, the United States deployed troops to the region in an attempt to pressure Iraq into conformity with Western interests. Kassem, however, persisted with his nationalist program. In 1959, he removed Iraq from the Baghdad Pact. Established in 1953, the Baghdad Pact was a NATO-sponsored agreement whose original members included Iraq, Iran, Pakistan, Turkey, and the United Kingdom. The purpose of the pact had been to contain "Nasirism," a socialist-derived form of Arab nationalism expounded by Egyptian president Abd-al-Nasir.

Throughout his brief reign as premier of the new Iraqi Republic, Kassem suppressed opposition and worked to bring about social reform. He attempted to remain neutral within the Cold War and was bitterly opposed to imperialism. It was his attempt to nationalize oil, however, that was most threatening to Western, and especially American, interests. In early 1963, Kassem had announced the formation of a national oil company to exploit the oil areas he had expropriated from foreign companies in 1961. The territory involved amounted to 99 percent of their concessionary areas. During an interview with *Le Monde* on February 4, Kassem said that he had received a threatening note from the U.S. State Department. Four days later, Kassem was toppled in a coup and eventually killed.[9]

For the next five years, Iraq was beset with internal strife, as various nationalist coalitions attempted to gain control of the country. In the end it was the Ba'ath (Resurrection) Party that gained power. Originating out of the struggle for national, postcolonial identity in Syria, the Ba'ath Party spread throughout Lebanon, Jordan, and Iraq. Socialist, secular, and modern in its orientation, the Ba'ath Party emerged as a dominant nationalist movement in the Middle East.[10]

It was during the late 1950s and 1960s that Saddam Hussein began to emerge as a powerful political force. In 1959 he had participated in the failed assassination attempt of Kassem; he was subsequently arrested and jailed until 1966. When the Ba'ath Party assumed control of Iraq in 1968, Saddam Hussein became vice president in charge of oil. Over the next few years, Saddam increasingly consolidated his power until, in 1979, he staged a "palace coup" and assumed full dictatorial control of the country.[11] Saddam attempted to become the uncontested leader of the Pan-Arab world, predicated on a nationalist and mostly secular ideology. Economically, he sought to industrialize the country, and to this end, he nationalized the Iraqi Petroleum Company in 1972. Hussein also attempted to negotiate between the two superpowers; however, his moves to the Soviet Union contributed to a hardening of U.S.–Iran relations.

The geopolitical terrain of the Middle East was radically altered in 1979. In February the U.S.-backed shah of Iran was deposed, and the subsequent Iranian revolution called for the creation of Islamic states throughout the Middle East. In particular, the Ayatollah Khomeini issued a call to abolish Arab or state nationalism in the interest of Islamic unity. Pointedly, this was a clear threat to the secular Iraqi government.

At this point, U.S. and Western interests were more concerned about the emergence of anti-Western theocracies throughout the region. In particular, Iran's new Islamic Republic began agitating against pro-U.S. oil sheikdoms in the Gulf. Of equal importance, however, was the fact that in November 1979, Islamic students seized the U.S. embassy in Tehran with Khomeini's blessing and took 52 Americans hostage for 444 days.

The history of the Middle East reveals a long series of conflicts between Iran and Iraq. Within the twentieth century, most conflicts have resulted from discrepancies over land boundaries and fluvial frontiers. Saddam Hussein saw the fall of the Shah of Iran and the ensuing revolution as an opportunity. In the political turmoil, Saddam hoped to put a halt to the Islamic Republic's destabilizing agitation and perhaps even topple the new regime before it had a chance to consolidate power. Moreover, Hussein saw this as an opportunity to capture Iran's southwest Khuzestan province, the heart of the country's oil industry. If successful, Iraqi oil production would increase from four to eleven million barrels a day, placing Baghdad in control of about 20 percent of world oil production and greatly increasing its global and regional leverage. Likewise, Iraq would gain possession of the Shatt al-Arab waterway. This channel is Iraq's only outlet to the sea; it also, though, provides access to Iran's oil refinery at Abadan. Following a 1937 treaty, Iraq assumed possession of the waterway; however, in 1969 the more powerful Iranian government took control of the Shatt al-Arab. Last, Iraq's decision to invade Iran was based on geopolitical concerns. Saddam understood that the United States was the most dominant power in the Gulf; accordingly he sought, through a mutual alliance against the ayatollah, to strengthen relations between Iraq and the United States.[12]

The United States did indeed find itself reversing its position and supporting the Hussein regime of Iraq in its war against Iran. Throughout the ensuing eight-year war, the United States funneled massive amounts of military arms, intelligence, and aid to Iraq. Crucially, in 1982 the Reagan administration removed Iraq from the list of countries labeled as supporters of terrorism—despite knowledge by U.S. officials that Saddam was employing chemical weapons against its Kurdish population and that Iraq was providing refuge to suspected Palestinian terrorists. Two years later the Reagan administration restored full diplomatic relations between Iraq and the United States; Iran was added to the list of terrorist states, thus denying it American products and severely limiting the supply of arms delivered to it by other countries.[13]

The military buildup of Iraq, however, began long before the American support of Hussein during the 1980s. Beginning in the 1950s, the Soviet Union was Iraq's chief arms supplier; France, likewise, was a longtime provider of arms. As Geoff Simons concludes, without the massive support—albeit sporadic and fluctuating—provided over the years by Britain, France, West Germany, the United States, the Soviet Union, and other countries, Saddam Hussein would never have been so well equipped for internal repression and for waging war against his neighbors.[14]

In 1988, United Nations negotiators arranged for a cease-fire, thereby bringing to an end the Iran–Iraq War. In retrospect, the war itself was indecisive. None of the major objectives specified by either Iran or Iraq were fulfilled: neither regime was overthrown, for example, and the sovereignty of the Shatt al-Arab remained in doubt. More significant is that the infrastructure of the two countries was severely damaged, particularly in the aftermath of the "war of the cities" in which both Iraq and Iran launched missile attacks on cities. Estimates placed the number of military deaths for Iran and Iraq at 260,000 and 105,000, respectively; civilian deaths, though, were believed to be over one million.

Jim Harding critically summarizes the geopolitics of Western intervention in Iraq specifically but the Middle East more broadly: "Through their support of coups and assassinations to protect Cold War and oil interests, the U.S., and Britain contributed to the political culture of violence within which Hussein rose to power."[15] More to the point, however, is the underlying motivation underscoring Western—but especially American—interests in the region. As both Simons and Larry Everest conclude, the U.S. support of the Hussein regime during the Iran–Iraq War was influenced, partially, out of Cold War ideologies. Indeed, the massive buildup of American and Soviet troops in the region during the Iran–Iraq War maybe triggered the only military confrontation between the two superpowers. However, the primary reason for Western support was economic. Throughout the Iran–Iraq War, the U.S. Commerce Department worked to facilitate business opportunities in Iraq. By the late 1980s U.S.–Iraq trade was worth billions, with dozens of Fortune 500 companies involved.[16]

Throughout the 1980s the United States supported, perhaps reluctantly, the Hussein-led Ba'ath Party. As discussed, the rationale for this support was a combination of capitalist opportunities and Cold War practicality—two elements that are more often than not mutually inclusive. However, following the collapse of the communist bloc beginning in 1989, the Cold War justification dissolved. Business opportunities would remain in the Middle East, but the Western powers would have more room to maneuver.

Saddam Hussein, for his part, would find himself fighting a second war—ushered in by his invasion of Kuwait—within two years of the cessation of hostilities with Iran. This new war was, at least from Saddam's perspective, justified on economic and territorial grounds. In 1990, the economy of Iraq was in ruins.

The rebuilding effort of Iraq was predicated on oil revenues. However, the Kuwaitis blatantly disregarded the OPEC-established quotas, thereby depressing oil prices. Hussein claimed that this practice amounted to a form of economic warfare. Ironically, Saudi Arabia and Kuwait had flooded the oil market during the preceding war in an effort to damage Iran's economy. Now the same economic weapon, as charged by Hussein, was being leveled against Iraq. Evidence also suggests that the United States was complicit with Kuwait in the manipulation of oil prices.[17]

Hussein further justified his invasion of Kuwait on the grounds that Kuwaiti territory—acquired through the delineation of the region's modern political boundaries in the 1920s—rightly belonged to Iraq. In addition, Saddam accused Kuwait of "slant drilling" into Iraq's Rumeila oil field. And last, Hussein had conducted his war against Iran, in part, on the pretext of a Pan-Arab platform. Following the cease-fire, he assumed, or hoped, that neighboring Arab states, including Kuwait and Saudi Arabia, would forgive the massive Iraqi debts incurred during the war. These requests, however, went unheeded.

Subsequent scholarship indicates that Saddam Hussein did not believe that the United States would intervene in its invasion and occupation of Kuwait; indeed, it is plausible that the Iraqi leader was in effect "entrapped" by an ambiguous American foreign policy. During the early months of 1990, Saddam met personally with five U.S. senators—Robert Dole, Alan Simpson, Howard Metzenbaum, James McClure, and Frank Murkowski. Also, based on a combination of established U.S.–Iraqi business interests, U.S. support during the war against Iran, and the refusal of the Bush Sr. administration to impose sanctions against Iraq (in light of human rights abuse charges), Hussein most likely concluded that Iraqi military intervention was acceptable—or at least not at odds with—U.S. geopolitical and economic interests.[18]

Following the Iraqi invasion, however, the Bush Sr. administration banned all trade to Iraq—with the exception of humanitarian assistance. Moreover, the United States advanced UN Security Resolution 660, which condemned the Iraqi invasion of Kuwait; demanded that Iraq withdraw immediately and unconditionally; and mandated that immediate negotiations be held between Iraq and Kuwait. Concurrently, the Bush Sr. administration began its campaign to mount an international alliance in support of military intervention to liberate Kuwait. An immediate hurdle was to convince the Saudi government to "request" U.S. protection against further Iraqi aggression. Although no evidence was forwarded to indicate that Hussein planned on invading Saudi Arabia, the Bush Sr. administration—through the efforts of U.S. secretary of defense Richard Cheney—was able to secure Saudi support. The Bush Sr. administration then concentrated on receiving assistance from Egypt to permit the aircraft carrier USS *Eisenhower* to gain access through the Suez Canal—a demand that went against a long-standing Egyptian policy of banning nuclear-powered ships or those carrying nuclear weapons from using the canal.[19]

Eventually, the Bush Sr. administration was able to muster an international coalition, often through the use of political or economic leverage. The U.S. government, for example, forgave $14 billion worth of Egyptian debts owed to the World Bank and arranged for other Western countries to likewise forgive or delay Egyptian debts. Military assistance and other forms of aid were promised to Turkey and Syria—despite the fact that Syria was still on the official American list of terrorist states. Even Iran was rewarded: following its agreement to aid the blockade of Iraq, loans from the U.S.-dominated World Bank were forthcoming. The Bush Sr. administration targeted especially the permanent members of the UN Security Council: the Soviet Union, in dire economic straits, received billions of dollars of aid; China (after abstaining on Resolution 678) received a substantial World Bank loan.[20]

Those governments that did not fall in line with the Bush Sr. administration's alliance building found themselves punished economically. Yemen, which voted against Resolution 678 (and abstained on Resolution 660) found that the United States stopped its $70 million aid program. Additionally, Yemen was hampered in its attempt to garner World Bank and International Monetary Fund loans, and Saudi Arabia expelled eight hundred thousand Yemeni workers. Elsewhere, the famine-stricken Sudan, which voiced support for Iraq, was denied food shipments, and Zimbabwe reluctantly changed its position from supporting Iraq to supporting the U.S.-led war when it was suggested to the Zimbabwean foreign minister that a projected International Monetary Fund loan would be blocked.[21]

Combat operations to remove Iraqi troops from Kuwait were quick and decisive. The Gulf War, however, left unresolved certain objectives of politicians. In particular, Saddam Hussein remained in power. The UN imposed sanctions in an attempt to render Iraq's military capabilities ineffective. The purported aim was to prevent Iraq from securing materials and technologies necessary for the manufacture of weapons of mass destruction. In actuality, these sanctions imposed a catastrophic loss of civilian life, as basic goods and services such as water and sanitation systems were unrestored following the decade-long warfare. The United States and United Kingdom likewise maintained and enforced, without UN authorization, "no-fly" zones in northern and southern Iraq. The purpose of these zones was supposedly to protect Kurdish minorities in the region as well as to maintain a control over the Iraqi military.

Following the 1992 presidential victory by William Clinton, the trend of U.S. foreign policy of capitalist expansion through the promotion of democracy and overseas markets continued. Discursively, the Clinton presidency emphasized "enlargement"—as opposed to the Cold War rhetoric of "containment"—as the prime goal of its foreign policy. Under this approach, the Clinton-era foreign policy was based on an attempt to achieve rapid economic growth through overseas trade and investment—in effect, an unreserved embrace of predatory globalization, with its adoption of a neoliberal version of minimally regulated capitalism.[22]

The United States, through the imposition of harsh sanctions and periodic bombings, continued to apply pressure on the Hussein regime. Effectively, however, these largely unilateral actions only intensified the hold that Hussein and the Ba'ath Party had over Iraq. Moreover, other European states, namely France and Russia, continued to call for an easing of sanctions while continuing to enforce Iraq's disarmament. Outside of the Clinton White House, several neoconservatives continue to press for the removal of Hussein—by force if necessary. United under the Washington think tank called Project for the New American Century, an open letter was sent in 1998 to Clinton, encouraging him to employ a preemptive strike against Iraq. The letter states,

> We are writing you because we are convinced that current American policy toward Iraq is not succeeding, and that we may soon face a threat in the Middle East more serious than any we have known since the end of the Cold War. . . . You have an opportunity to chart a clear and determined course for meeting this threat. We urge you to seize that opportunity, and to enunciate a new strategy that would secure the interests of the U.S. and our friends and allies around the world. That strategy should aim . . . at the removal of Saddam Hussein's regime from power.[23]

In a call for unilateral and military action, the letter continues, "We can no longer depend on our partners in the Gulf War coalition to continue to uphold the sanctions or to punish Saddam when he blocks or evades UN inspections." Moreover, "if Saddam does acquire the capability to deliver weapons of mass destruction, as he is almost certain to do if we continue along the present course, the safety of American troops in the region, of our friends and allies like Israel and the moderate Arab states, and a significant portion of the world's supply of oil will all be put at hazard." The letter also states, "We believe the U.S. has the authority under existing UN resolutions to take the necessary steps, including military steps, to protect our vital interests in the Gulf. In any case, American policy cannot continue to be crippled by a misguided insistence on unanimity in the UN Security Council."[24] In other words, signatories to the letter believed that it was in America's best interest to pursue a unilateral and militarist strategy to remove Saddam Hussein. The letter was signed by eighteen members of the Project for the New American Century, including Donald Rumsfeld (who would become secretary of defense under Bush), Paul Wolfowitz (defense deputy), Peter Rodman (assistant secretary of defense for international security affairs), William Schneider (chairman of the Pentagon's Defense Science Board), Richard Perle (chair of the Defense Policy Board), Richard Armitage (deputy secretary of state), Paula Dobriansky (undersecretary of state for global affairs), John Bolton (undersecretary of state for arms control and international security), Zalmay Khalilzad (special assistant to the president for Near East, South West Asian, and North African affairs), and Elliott Abrams (National Security Council and presidential advisor for the Middle East). In short, the open letter was, in the words of Harding, to become the doctrine of Pax Americana, constructed by a select assemblage of men and women who were to become the most powerful group within the Bush administration.[25]

OPERATION IRAQI FREEDOM

On March 19, 2003, the U.S.-led invasion of Iraq began. Military intervention was quickly justified when, at 10:16 PM (eastern standard time), Bush addressed the American public. During his four-minute televised appearance, Bush explained that "coalition forces [were] in the early stages of military operations to disarm Iraq, to free its people and to defend the world from grave danger." References to "coalition forces" permeated the declaration, as Bush reaffirmed that "every nation in this coalition has chosen to bear the duty and share the honor of serving in our common defense." Bush concluded that America was "helping Iraqis achieve a united, stable and free country," one that will "require our sustained commitment." This last phrase, "sustained commitment," would assume monumental proportions in the months to come.[26]

The war was rapid. By April 6, coalition forces had isolated Baghdad. Within a week, on April 14, Pentagon officials indicated that major combat operations were over. And in just two more weeks, on May 1, Bush declared an end to combat operations.

The war was justified on the pretext of a moral responsibility to free the world from an imminent threat. Direct military intervention, however, also brought to a close months of intense and, retrospectively, largely futile political negotiations to prevent war. In the months preceding the invasion of Iraq, the Bush administration discursively constructed a justification for war. Underscoring this justification, though, was the continuation of a long-standing policy of regional hegemony. As the research of Bob Woodward makes clear—and his work is based on numerous interviews with Bush and members of Bush's administration—the war was, for all intents and purposes, a *fait accompli*.[27] The underlying purpose was, in actions if not words, to expand the economic and military interests of the United States. This is shown clearly, for example, by the way the Bush administration proceeded to act as an occupying government. On September 21, 2003, Paul Bremer, U.S. head of the Coalition Provisional Authority, signed new laws for Iraq's economy. Immediately the economic was to be opened up to foreign investment as all previous state-run businesses could be purchased abroad. This included health care, education, municipal services, and nearly all public utilities. The oil industry, while not entirely foreign owned, would be dominated by outside partners. Banks in Iraq could likewise be foreign controlled from 50 to 100 percent. Before Iraq had established a constitution and before it was to have elections, the United States unilaterally (Britain was not consulted) structured Iraq's economy for years to come.[28]

The Bush administration planned to invade Iraq and foment "regime change" with or without the support of the United Nations. This attitude conformed with an established pattern of unilateralism within American foreign policy. Since assuming office, the Bush administration withdrew from the 1972 Antiballistic Missile Treaty; unsigned the Treaty of Rome, which created the International Criminal Court; and even claimed itself no longer bound by the 1969 Vienna Convention on the Law of Treaties, which requires signatory nations to refrain from taking steps to undermine treaties they sign. The Bush administration removed the United States from the Kyoto Protocol on Global Warming, refused to support attempts to strengthen the Biological Weapons Convention, and walked out (with Israel) of the United Nations conference on racism.[29] This "go-it-alone" attitude to foreign policy constitutes one component of the Bush administration's manifest destiny of the twenty-first century—an interesting attitude given the prominent rhetoric of the Coalition of the Willing. I return to this point later.

Ideologically, the foreign policy approach of the Bush administration is based on a realist political thinking best labeled *hegemonist*. As discussed by Ivo Daalder and James Lindsay, this philosophy rests on five propositions. First, it is assumed that the United States is enmeshed within a dangerous world, a Hobbesian environment that is characterized by evil. The perils that America faces abroad—whether in the form of Iraq, China, North Korea, or unspecified "rogue" states—permeate the speeches of Bush, Cheney, Condoleezza Rice, and Rumsfeld. Second, self-interested nation-states are assumed to be the key actors in world politics. Indeed, it is significant to note that the Bush administration rarely mentions "globalization"; neither is the demise of the nation-state ever contemplated, as many globalization theorists argue. Crucially, Macapagal-Arroyo does forward a geopolitical vision of globalization, one that is discordant with much of the Bush rhetoric. Third, power politics is the rule of the game. Furthermore, power is about more than capability; it must be used to be effective. For the Bush administration, credibility was predicated on the demonstration of power; consequently, if America leads, others would follow.[30]

The fourth basic proposition of the hegemonist worldview is that multilateral agreements and institutions are neither essential nor necessarily conducive to American interests. As such, the Coalition of the Willing was a necessary "evil" for the Bush administration in its pursuit of its unilateral agenda. Members of the Bush administration, especially Rice and Bush, viewed agreements such as the aforementioned treaties as constraining the United States. Relatedly, the fifth proposition is that the United States, as viewed by the Bush administration, is a unique great power. This proposition is in some respects antithetical to the realist worldview, which treats the internal makeup and character of states as irrelevant.[31] However, as discussed in the following, this element is crucial to the discursive constructions of the Bush administration's Will to War.

How are we to interpret the increased unilateralism of the United States? What are the justifications and potential consequences of such a course of action, including the decision to go to war? These are questions that have received considerable attention. Some works, such as those by Peter Singer, Richard Falk, David Domke, and Jean Elshtain, address the philosophical and moral implications.[32] Others focus more closely on the political economy and concentrate on the materiality of past and present policies. The writings of David Harvey, Phyllis Bennis, Michael Mann, and Alex Callinicos fall under this category.[33] At this point I deviate slightly from these lines of inquiry. My primary concern is not with the veracity or validity of the Bush administration's justification for war. Rather, my interest lies in the foreign policies of other governments, namely the Philippines, that were situated within the context of Pax Americana.

It becomes necessary, therefore, to consider more closely the Bush administration's *casus belli*, America's Will to War. But it is imperative to recognize, as David Domke details, that the War on Terror was perceived by Bush as being of divine origin. Bush's Will to War, specifically, was God's will.

AMERICAN MESSIANISM AND TERROR

We can also be confident in the ways of providence, even when they are far from our understanding. Events aren't moved by blind change and chance. Behind all of life and all of history,

there's a dedication and purpose, set by the hand of a just and
faithful God. And that hope will never be shaken.[34]

Bush has consistently presented himself as carrying out God's will in the
conduct of both the War on Terror and its related "battles" in Afghanistan
and Iraq. During his September 20, 2001, speech, Bush explained, "In our
grief and anger, we have found our mission and our moment." These two
terms—*mission* and *moment*—were recurrent throughout the Bush's subsequent speeches and provided the basis for preemption. Bush, in effect, announced that he was doing God's will and, having been shown the path, determined that immediate action was required. Bush pronounced, "I will not
yield; I will not rest; I will not relent in waging this struggle for freedom
and security for the American people."[35] In his 2002 State of the Union address, Bush explained, "After America was attacked, it was if our entire
country looked into a mirror and saw our better selves." Further, "We have
glimpsed what a new culture of responsibility could look like. We want to
be a nation that serves goals larger than self. We've been offered a unique
opportunity, and we must not let this moment pass."[36] As part of the greater
War on Terror, a new era of manifest destiny emerged, one that afforded
"unique opportunities" to further American hegemony. But crucially, this
was perceived by Bush and his cabinet as a "fleeting" opportunity: *We must
not let this moment pass.*

That Bush assumed the figure of a prophet is not unique in American
politics. Neither are his intonations that he is answering God's call. Numerous presidents have assumed this rhetorical style. Rather, the political fundamentalism of Bush is an extension of a long-standing tradition in American politics, namely that of the jeremiad. A recurrent theme of American
politics—one effectively promoted by the Bush administration—has been
that of America as the beacon of freedom. President Andrew Jackson referred to U.S. expansion as "extending the area of freedom"; President
William McKinley (responsible for America's occupation of the Philippines)
declared, "We intervene [in the Philippines] not for conquest. We intervene
for humanity's sake [and to] earn the praises of every lover of freedom the
world over"; in the context of World War II, President Franklin Roosevelt
said, "We fight not for conquest, but for a world in which this nation and
all that this nation represents will be safe for our children;" and during the
Cold War, President Harry Truman explained, "If we falter in our leadership we may endanger the peace of the world and we shall surely endanger
the welfare of this nation."[37]

Common within an American jeremiad tradition is the view of the United States as the Promised Land. People in the United States have long believed that America was set apart from the rest of the world. Historians have argued that this attitude is derived, in part, from the founding of the country as the first republic since classical times. Additionally, the mixture of Puritanism and liberalism of the early settlers contributed to an "American Exceptionalism." Americans were convinced that they were a beacon to mankind and began to see themselves as a chosen people.[38]

Bush has referred to the exceptionalism of America on numerous occasions. As one example, during the 2000 presidential campaign, Bush said, "Our nation is chosen by God and commissioned by history to be a model to the world of justice."[39] "America" is thus conceived as more than an objective geographic or political designation; rather, it has been and continues to be constructed as a powerful symbol charged with cultural meaning. It is a mythical space; the setting in which humanity's dreams are realized.[40]

America, consequently, has been defined not by a set of ideologies but rather as an ideology itself. The key principles of Americanism include liberty, equality, individualism, populism, and limited government. As Clyde Prestowitz writes, seeing themselves as a chosen people laboring in God's vineyard to create a new, perfect society, Americans find in these values their true religion.[41] When Bush addressed the nation the night of September 11, 2001, he said, "Our way of life, our very freedom came under attack." It was not the World Trade Center or the Pentagon that was attacked; it was not New York or Washington, D.C. Indeed, it was not even America per se that was attacked. In this sense, to say otherwise would be redundant, for America signifies freedom. Moreover, Bush focused more on the importance of these signifiers—liberty, freedom, and opportunity— than he did the concrete or literal landscape. He explained, "Terrorist attacks can shake the foundations of our biggest buildings, but they cannot touch the foundation of America. These acts shattered steel, but they cannot dent the steel of American resolve." Bush is saying, in effect, that we can reconstruct the buildings; the more pressing issue is the *image* of the United States.[42]

Americans have been constructed as the exception; concurrently, however, this exceptionalism has been twinned with a sense of moral obligation and responsibility to bring the rest of the world within its fold. As Howard-Pitney summarizes, "No belief has been more central to American civil religion that the idea that Americans are in some important sense a chosen people with a historic mission to save and remake the world."[43]

This remaking would consist of American values, including freedom, democracy, and liberty.

The idea of freedom, as it developed in the American setting, has always entailed a sense of moral duty and responsibility. This is derived, in part, from the seventeenth-century liberalism of John Locke. This is also derived from the Puritan heritage. The Puritan exile to the "New World," is based on a reading of the Old Testament. The example of Moses and the covenant made clear that escape into freedom involved hardship and sacrifice; in short, freedom was made a sacred concept, one that demanded a consensus to its nature and its requirements.[44] It is not coincidental that Bush, in the aftermath of the September 11 attacks, declared, "Freedom and fear are at war. The advance of human freedom—the great achievement of our time, and the great hope of every time—now depends on us. Our nation—this generation—will lift a dark threat of violence from our people and our future. We will rally the world to this cause by our efforts, by our courage." It is significant that Bush indicates that although freedom is the hope of every generation, it has been America—and the present generation—that has *achieved* human freedom. On this account, America is once again constructed as the Chosen Nation, composed of Chosen People, who must rally the world in a monumental clash of good and evil. Prestowitz notes that when American leaders promise to promote the spread of freedom globally, what they have in mind is Americanism.[45]

In short, prophetic discourse seeks to reshape, to re-create the audience in accordance with a strict set of ideas as commanded by God, revealed in natural law, and assented to in principle but unrealized by the audience.[46] The speeches of Bush are thus presented as containing the word of God. Moreover, to be a prophet, it is not enough for one to speak on behalf of an absolute truth; instead, there must be a sense of overwhelming threat. During times of crises, when it appears as if the entire world is hurtling toward Armageddon, the prophet, through his deliverance of God's word, brings order and sensibility. The prophet assumes the dual roles of accuser and judge: the prophet is called into being when the law has been violated. And once assuming this role, the prophet announces the charges and the verdict of God against the transgressors.[47] In effect, this is the presumed position of Bush. In his address of September 20, 2001, Bush declared, "[The terrorists] hate our freedoms—our freedom of religion, our freedom of speech, our freedom to vote and assemble and disagree with each other." Bush continued that the terrorists "want to overthrow existing governments in many Muslim countries . . . . They want to drive Israel out of the Middle East. They want to drive Christians and Jews out of vast regions of Asia and Africa." He then equated the terrorists with other "murderous ideologies of the 20th century," including "fascism, and Nazism, and totalitarianism." Having thus identified the transgressions, Bush announced the verdict: "Americans should not expect one battle, but a lengthy campaign.... It may include dramatic strikes, visible on TV, and covert operations, secret even in success. We will starve terrorists of funding, turn them one against another, drive them from place to place ... and we will pursue nations that provide aid or safe haven to terrorism." Bush emphasized, "The only way to defeat terrorism as a threat to our way of life is to stop it, eliminate it, and destroy it where it grows." Bush concluded, "The course of this conflict is not known, yet its outcome is certain. Freedom and fear, justice and cruelty, have always been at war, and we know that God is not neutral between them."[48]

Prestowitz concludes that the effect of America's religiosity has been to make the contest a moral crusade. Because Americans are expected to act in accord with their consciences, they find it difficult to support what seems to be an unjust war or one fought for mundane or self-interested reasons. This accounts for necessity of knowing that one's loved one did not die in vain. There must be a purpose in death. To endorse a war, Americans must see themselves on God's side, fighting for good against evil.[49] These attitudes toward war and death, of course, are not unique to the United States. Most, if not all, governments attempt to justify the necessity of war. That said, questions of the justness of war are answered differently within the Coalition of the Willing. In the following section, I detail the public pronouncements by the Bush administration regarding the necessity of military force in Iraq.

CASUS BELLI

The speeches by Bush, Rumsfeld, Colin Powell, and the rest of the administration constructed a particular "truthful" narrative, one that was presented to the American public, the United Nations, and the "international community" as a whole. In effect, the Bush administration was forwarding its Will to War. And these were the truths on which citizens and governments were to decide. According to the Bush discourse, there was no middle ground, no alternative path. Unlike the Cold War, the Bush pronouncement was a preemptive strike against the possibility of a nonaligned movement. Either one joined the United States as part of the Coalition of the Willing, or, as implied in Matthew 12:30, one would be scattered throughout the world. On what basis, therefore, did the United States construct the conflict?

The Bush administration's initial case for war was based on the claim that the UN Security Council had required Saddam Hussein to rid Iraq of its weapons of mass destruction. U.S. officials argued, however, that Hussein willingly and flagrantly violated UN resolutions. Accordingly, the Bush administration justified military intervention on the grounds of the November 2002 UN Security Resolution 1441, which required Hussein to comply with UN disarmament obligations or face serious consequences, namely war. However, Resolution 1441 explicitly stated that only the Security Council was able to decide when and what steps may be required for the implementation of the resolution and to secure peace and security in the region. The Bush administration was not, therefore, justified to unilaterally take action against Iraq. As Singer summarizes, under Resolution 1441 the Security Council had retained the right to make that decision itself and to decide on the nature of the consequences that would follow if Iraq was found to be in violation of its obligations. This is the reason why the Bush administration tried so hard to obtain a second resolution declaring that Iraq had not disarmed and authorizing the use of force against Iraq. This also accounts for the reluctance of some governments to support the Bush administration's Coalition of the Willing.[50]

A second *casus belli* was that Iraq, having failed to disarm, posed an imminent threat to the security of the United States. During the weeks leading up to war, considerable documentary evidence was provided to support the Bush administration's claim that Iraq was capable of launching biological or chemical attacks within forty-five minutes and that it had, or was very close to having, nuclear weapons capabilities. In his 2002 State of the Union address, Bush explained, "Iraq continues to flaunt its hostility toward America and to support terror. The Iraqi regime has plotted to develop anthrax, and nerve gas, and nuclear weapons for over a decade. This is a regime that has already used poison gas to murder thousands of its own citizens— leaving the bodies of mothers huddled over their dead children. This is a regime that agreed to international inspections—then kicked out the inspectors. This is a regime that has something to hide from the civilized world."[51] Discursively, Bush reveals a considerable amount of information in this statement. First he states that the Iraqi regime has weapons and that it has used these weapons in the past. Second, through his description of mothers huddled over dead children, he implicitly warns that civilians are not spared by the Iraqi regime. And third, his phrase that the Iraqi regime has something to hide is suggestive of a parent scolding a small child. Little children who are caught in a lie have something to hide.

The Bush administration, despite UN Resolution 1441, declared emphatically that it was justified to act preemptively. Identified later as the "Bush doctrine," Bush announced in June 2002 that the United States was within its right to use any and all means to ensure the security of its territorial integrity and all of its citizens. In effect, the Bush doctrine upheld the sanctity of the U.S. nation-state above all others. On August 26, 2003, Vice President Cheney applied the new preemptive strike and unilateralist doctrine to Iraq, arguing, "What we must not do in the face of a mortal threat is to give in to wishful thinking or willful blindness. . . . The risks of inaction are far greater than the risks of action."[52]

The Bush doctrine became official policy when the White House released its 2002 *National Security Strategy*. The aggressiveness of the doctrine is made clear in the statement that the United States "will not hesitate to act alone, if necessary, to exercise [its] right of self-defense by acting preemptively . . . against terrorists." Although this attitude has, in some respects, always been understood, the overt nature of placing it in a public document illustrated the growing militarism of the Bush administration. Within the *National Security Strategy,* Bush wrote, "As a matter of common sense and self-defense, America will act against such emerging threats before they are fully formed. We cannot defend America and our friends by hoping for the best. So we must be prepared to defeat our enemies' plans, using the best intelligence and proceeding with deliberate action. History will judge harshly those who saw this coming danger but failed to act. In the new world we have entered, the only path to peace and security is the path of action."[53] As Domke concludes, the language of imminent action was central to the Bush administration's justification of a preemptive policy; for Christian fundamentalists, this constant perception of limited time impels imminent action and, in a related manner, unremitting calls for more action on behalf of their causes.[54]

Connected with the discourse of imminent threat, the Bush administration likewise forwarded a linkage between the Iraqi government and the War on Terror. This discourse was initially forward to the public when Iraq was identified as part of the Axis of Evil. In the buildup to war, Bush and other members of his administration further justified this cause through explicit links between Saddam's regime and al Qaeda. During an eight-day period (October 28 to November 4, 2002), for example, Bush made this claim in eleven separate speeches.[55] Rhetorically, the War on Terror would become a major impetus for the construction of the coalition. Indeed, as the writings of Woodward, Bennis, and Domke indicate, the Bush administration consciously used the threat of terror as a justification for its long-standing goal of removing Hussein. The devastating attacks of September 11, 2001, simply provided a "just" cause. As Harding concludes, "It is now irrefutable that 9/11 was an excuse for the Bush administration to launch its Pax Americana campaign. In the aftershock of 9/11, National Security Advisor Condoleeza Rice encouraged members of the National Security Council 'to capitalize on these opportunities to fundamentally change American doctrine' and Rumsfeld called for an immediate attack on Iraq."[56]

Last, a final justification for war hinged on the liberation of the Iraqi people. Speaking before the United Nations in September 2002, Bush announced that the quest for liberty for the Iraqi people was a great moral cause and a great strategic goal. Couched under the rubric of "humanitarian intervention," the Bush administration forwarded the argument that military action was required to remove a brutal, ruthless dictator. Certainly the goal of liberating peoples from a ruthless dictator resonated with the professed ethics of Bush. However, it is worth considering that a discourse of liberation sits uneasily with the pronounced political realism of the Bush administration. This component is best seen in a *Foreign Affairs* article written by Condoleezza Rice, one year before she became Bush's national security advisor. I quote at length:

> Power matters, both the exercise of power by the United States and the ability of others to exercise it. Yet many in the United States are (and have always been) uncomfortable with the notions of power politics, great powers, and power balances. In an extreme form, this discomfort leads to a reflexive appeal instead to notions of international law and norms, and the belief that the support of many states—or even better, of institutions like the United Nations—is essential to the legitimate exercise of power. The 'national interest' is replaced with 'humanitarian interests' or the interests of the 'international community.' . . . To be sure, there is nothing wrong with doing something that benefits all humanity, but that is, in a sense, a second-order effect. America's pursuit of the national interest will create conditions that promote freedom, markets, and peace. . . . U.S. intervention in . . . 'humanitarian' crises should be, at best, exceedingly rare. This does not mean that the United States must ignore humanitarian and civil conflicts around the world. But the military cannot be involved everywhere.[57]

Recognizing the limitations of even the most powerful military in the world, Rice acknowledges that the United States cannot respond to all crises. A government must be selective, and it must do so based first and foremost on its own self-preservation: security. Given the recurrence of "humanitarian crises" that exist, including famines, civil wars, and genocides, Rice states that the deployment of U.S. troops must be determined by American national interests. These may, of course, include resources, strategic areas, or some other geopolitical or economic objective.

This sense of political realism underlying the Will to War is of the utmost importance with respect to coalition building. It suggests that other governments *may* likewise base their decision not out of any sense of moral responsibility but instead out of a sense of potential gain. Likewise, governments may choose not to be part of a coalition because of perceived strategic losses rather than moral outrage.

COALITION BUILDING

Much is made of American's "turn" toward "unilateralism." Rightly so. But unilateralism, even if supported by (arguably) the world's most dominant military force, will always be constrained. This stems not so much with genuine concern for the welfare of other governments—although this may indeed occur—but rather by the need to utilize potential air space, navigate maritime straits and canals, or eliminate the possibility of other threats. Even if a government seeks war unilaterally, it will generally "test the waters" so to speak and call on other governments for assistance in some form. Coalition building, even for the "lone superpower," is still a necessary component of political and military strategy.

In the weeks following the attacks on the Pentagon and the World Trade Center, the Bush administration began to construct a Coalition of the Willing. This alliance was necessary for two reasons. First, despite the unilateral and militarist trajectory of the United States, it was clear to Bush, Rumsfeld, and General Tommy Franks that cooperation of other countries was required: overflight paths and staging grounds needed to be obtained. Additionally, though this would not be definitive until the days immediately preceding the invasion, an international "coalition" was symbolically important in light of not receiving UN Security Council authorization for war. As indicated in chapter 1, such a multilateral alliance could be constructed to deflect criticisms of American unilateralism.

On September 27, 2001, speaking before an audience of airline employees at Chicago's O'Hare Airport, Bush discussed the coalition. He said, "There is a broad coalition of nations that understand what's at stake that have come rallying to our side. And I want to thank the nations of the world that have stood side-by-side with our country to defend freedom. It's heartening to know that we stand not alone in the world." Different governments would perform various functions in this coalition, the president explained. "It's a coalition that will require different efforts from different countries. Some countries may want to participate in one way, but not in another. All we ask is that you participate. All we ask is that you use the same amount of effort the United States will to win this war against freedom, to win this battle against global terrorism." He continued: "This coalition will exist to achieve the mission, and I can assure you our mission will not change to fit any coalition's." In other words, Bush laid the path, and others may follow. But deviation would not be permitted. Bush continued: "America will stand strong. Others will tire and weary. . . . Others will second-guess, but not our nation. Others will become impatient, but not this great nation. . . . We hope everybody follows, but we're marching on." The message was clear. The Bush administration identified its mission—to lead the other nations of the world, be they willing or not, to freedom and salvation from evil. There would be no space for discussion; there would be no time for debate; there would be no middle ground. The coalition, by implication, would consist of those nations that were good, strong, and willing to follow orders. The Philippines, initially, appeared to fall in line.

NOTES

1. Office of the Press Secretary, "Statement by the President in His Address to the Nation," September 11, 2001, www.whitehouse.gov/releases/2001/09/2001 0911–16.html (July 27, 2004); Peter Singer, *The President of Good and Evil: The Ethics of George W. Bush* (New York: Dutton, 2004), 143.

2. David Domke, *God Willing? Political Fundamentalism in the White House, the "War on Terror," and the Echoing Press* (London: Pluto Press, 2004), 3.

3. Office of the Press Secretary, "Address to the Nation."

4. Singer, *Good and Evil*, 142.

5. Office of the Press Secretary, "Address to the Nation"; Office of the Press Secretary, "Address to a Joint Session of Congress and the American People," September 20, 2001, www.whitehouse.gov/news/releases/2001/09/20010920–8.html (July 27, 2004).

6. Murray Edelman, *Political Language: Words That Succeed and Politics That Fail* (New York: Academic Press, 1977), 45.

7. Michel Foucault, "Truth and Power," in *Power/Knowledge: Selected Interviews and Other Writings, 1972–1977*, ed. C. Gordon, trans. C. Gordon, L. Marshall, J. Mepham, and K. Soper (New York: Pantheon Books, 1980), 109–33 (quote on 132).

8. Foucault, "Truth and Power," 131–32.

9. Geoff Simons, *Iraq: From Sumer to Post-Saddam* (New York: Palgrave MacMillan, 2004), 258–59.

10. Jim Harding, *After Iraq: War, Imperialism, and Democracy* (London: Merlin Press, 2004), 8–9.

11. Harding, *After Iraq*, 9–10.

12. Simons, *From Sumer to Post-Saddam*; Larry Everest, *Oil, Power, and Empire: Iraq and the U.S. Global Agenda* (Monroe, Maine: Common Courage Press, 2004), 95.

13. Simons, *From Sumer to Post-Saddam*, 322.

14. Simons, *From Sumer to Post-Saddam*, 318.

15. Harding, *After Iraq*, 11.

16. Simons, *From Sumer to Post-Saddam*, 325–28; Everest, *Oil, Power, and Empire*.

17. Simons, *From Sumer to Post-Saddam*, 343.

18. For a detailed discussion of the negotiations leading up to the invasion, see Lawrence Freedman and Efraim Karsh, *The Gulf Conflict 1990–1991: Diplomacy and War in the New World Order* (Princeton, N.J.: Princeton University Press, 1993).

19. Simons, *From Sumer to Post-Saddam*, 354–55; see also Phyllis Bennis, *Before and After: U.S. Foreign Policy and the War on Terrorism* (New York: Olive Branch Press, 2003).

20. Simons, *From Sumer to Post-Saddam*, 355–57.

21. Simons, *From Sumer to Post-Saddam*, 358.

22. Richard Falk, *The Great Terror War* (New York: Olive Branch Press, 2003).

23. Project for the New American Century, "Open Letter to President Clinton," www.newamericancentury.org/iraqclintonletter.htm (accessed April 27, 2004).

24. Project for the New American Century, "Open Letter."

25. Harding, *After Iraq*, 34.

26. Office of the Press Secretary, "President Bush Addresses the Nation," March 19, 2003, www.whitehouse.gov/news/releases/2003/03/2030219.17.html (April 12, 2004).

27. Bob Woodward, *Plan of Attack* (New York: Simon & Shuster, 2004).

28. Harding, *After Iraq*, 142.

29. Chalmers Johnson, *The Sorrows of Empire: Militarism, Secrecy, and the End of the Republic* (New York: Henry Holt, 2004), 72–77.

30. Ivo H. Daalder and James M. Lindsay, *America Unbound: The Bush Revolution in Foreign Policy* (Washington, D.C.: Brookings Institution Press, 2003), 40–44.

31. Daalder and Lindsay, *America Unbound*, 44–45.

32. Singer, *Good and Evil*; Falk, *Terror War*; Domke, *God Willing?*; Jean Bethke Elshtain, *Just War against Terror: The Burden of American Power in a Violent World* (New York: Basic Books, 2003).

33. David Harvey, *The New Imperialism* (Oxford: Oxford University Press, 2003); Bennis, *Before and After*; Alex Calinicos, *The New Mandarins of American Power* (Cambridge: Polity Press, 2003); Michael Mann, *Incoherent Empire* (New York: Verso, 2003).

34. Remarks by George W. Bush at the National Prayer Breakfast, quoted in Domke, *God Willing?* 63.

35. Office of the Press Secretary, "Address to the Nation."

36. Office of the Press Secretary, "President Delivers [2002] State of the Union Address," January 29, 2002, www.whitehouse.gov/releases/2002/01/20020129–11.html (April 12, 2004).

37. Clyde Prestowitz, *Rogue Nation: American Unilateralism and the Failure of Good Intentions* (New York: Basic Books, 2003), 30–33.

38. Prestowitz, *Rogue Nation*, 31.

39. Domke, *God Willing?* 63.

40. David Howard-Pitney, *The Afro-American Jeremiad: Appeals for Justice in America* (Philadelphia: Temple University Press, 1990), 5.

41. Prestowitz, *Rogue Nation*, 36.

42. Office of the Press Secretary, "Address to Nation"; Prestowitz, *Rogue Nation*, 36.

43. Howard-Pitney, *Afro-American Jeremiad*, 6.

44. James F. Darsey, *The Prophetic Tradition and Radical Rhetoric in America* (New York: New York University Press, 1997), 201.

45. Prestowitz, *Rogue Nation*, 36.

46. Darsey, *Prophetic Tradition*, 202.

47. Darsey, *Prophetic Tradition*, 24.

48. Office of the Press Secretary, "Address to Joint Session and American People."

49. Prestowitz, *Rogue Nation*, 41.

50. Singer, *Good and Evil*, 159.

51. Office of the Press Secretary, "2002 State of the Union Address."

52. Douglas Kellner, *From 9/11 to Terror War: The Dangers of the Bush Legacy* (Lanham, Md.: Rowman & Littlefield, 2003), 20.

53. *National Security Strategy of the United States of America*, 2002, www.whitehouse.gov/nsc/nssall.html (March 31, 2004).

54. Domke, *God Willing?* 86.

55. Singer, *Good and Evil*, 257.

56. Harding, *After Iraq*, 145.

57. Condoleeza Rice, "Campaign 2000—Promoting the National Interest," *Foreign Affairs* 79 (2000), www.foreignpolicy2000.org/library/issuebriefs/readingnotes/fa_rice.html (July 28, 2004).

4

WORKING FOR SOLIDARITY

So give your servant a discerning heart to govern your people
and to distinguish between right and wrong. For who is able to govern
this great people of yours?

1 Kings 3:9

On November 20, 2001, in the immediate aftermath of the attacks on
the World Trade Center and the Pentagon, President Bush and President Macapagal-Arroyo issued a joint statement reaffirming the "strength
and warmth of bilateral relations." They did so on the fiftieth anniversary of
the signing of the U.S.–Philippine Mutual Defense Treaty. In their statement, Bush expressed his gratification to the Philippines for their efforts in
the War on Terror. Both presidents acknowledged poverty as a contributing
factor to terrorism and thus the necessity of promoting economic growth
and development.[1]

The two presidents resolved to work closely to expand trade bilater-
ally, regionally, and globally. Bush also agreed to work with Congress to provide the Philippines with over $1 billion in benefits based on a generalized
system of preferences, increased quotas on U.S. importation of textiles and
apparels, and a special line of credit worth $200 million for private invest-
ment. In short, Macapagal-Arroyo was "rewarded" by Bush for her "commitment to fight poverty, accelerate economic reform, enhance transparency
and promote good governance." Bush also acknowledged her leadership in
the fight against terrorism within the Philippines and against international
terrorist networks.[2]

Two years later, in October 2003, Bush made a brief visit to the Philippines. During a photo opportunity held at Malacañang Palace in Manila,

Macapagal-Arroyo thanked Bush for his coming to the Philippines, noting, "It affirms the warm and deep relations between our two countries. It's another building block in the revitalized and maturing alliance, rooted in shared histories and shared values, a common interest in global peace and prosperity, as well as a real commitment of combating terrorism and advancing freedom." Macapagal-Arroyo used the occasion to reaffirm America's support for the Philippines as a nonpermanent member of the UN Security Council and for being designated as a major non-NATO ally. She then identified the "assistance" provided by the United States, including a $50 million investment from Ford to launch the Philippines as an export hub and $33 million of new USAID (U.S. Agency for International Development) money for educational assistance in conflict-affected areas of the Philippines.[3]

Bush, in turn, thanked the Philippine president for her support in the War on Terror and for contributing to the effort to promote freedom and liberty throughout the world. Bush said to Macapagal-Arroyo, "You've been strong and stalwart, and that's what's needed. The terrorists want to frighten people into inaction. They want to create fear, and therefore, have their way. And you have—you've been strong. And I appreciate that very much. We want to continue to help you." Noting the desire to work together on matters of education and other ways to "enhance democracy," Bush continued, "I also want to thank you for your vision of [understanding] that freedom is important, it's a human right, and where there's human suffering and tyranny, that . . . the free world must work to change conditions, hopefully in peaceful ways, but sometimes tyranny is so stubborn and ignores the reality, that we have to make tough decisions."[4]

Bush addressed the Philippine Congress during his visit. On this occasion, the president discussed the long-standing relations between the Philippines and the United States. He began with reference to Jose Rizal, an *ilustrado* who became a martyr in the Philippines' quest for independence against the Spanish monarch in the nineteenth century. Bush noted, "The great patriot, Jose Rizal, said that nations win their freedom by deserving it, by loving what is just, what is good, what is great to the point of dying for it. In the 107 years since that good man's heroic death, Filipinos have fought for justice, you have sacrificed for democracy—you have earned your freedom." Bush then moved to World War II, saying, "Our soldiers liberated the Philippines from colonial rule. Together we rescued the islands from invasion and occupation. The names of Bataan, Corregidor, Leyte Luzon evoke the memories of shared struggle and shared loss and shared victory." Bush continued, "Along the way and through the years, Americans have gained an abiding respect for the character of your nation and for the decency and courage of the Filipino people."[5]

As indicated in chapter 1, a mendicant patriarchalism continues to typify U.S.–Philippine international relations. As detailed by Anthony Woodiwiss, political leaders before and after independence begged the Americans for favors so that the former could, in turn, respond to those who were also begging favors. The Philippine–U.S. relationship has thus historically been founded on a dependency, with Philippine leaders looking up, expectantly, to their "benevolent" tutors.[6]

In certain respects the mendicity evinced by Macapagal-Arroyo conforms readily with the jeremiad rhetoric of Bush. In this context, Bush assumes the father figure—the prophet—who looms above the masses of Filipinos, ready to deliver them to the Promised Land of opportunities. In his remarks to the Philippine Congress, for example, Bush reiterated the commitment that is required in combating terrorism and spreading peace throughout the world. Bush also applauded the Philippines, as a father might to a child, in the government's effort to modernize and reform its military, and he affirmed that the United States would provide technical assistance and field expertise and funding.[7]

As benevolent leader of the free world, Bush acknowledged the assistance of the Philippine people toward Iraq. "Americans and Filipinos," he said, "and many others share a common vision for that country. Coalition forces, including Filipino peacekeepers and medical workers, are working for the rise of freedom and self-government in Iraq. We're helping to build a free Iraq, because the long-suffering Iraqi people deserve lives of opportunity and dignity. And we're helping to build a free Iraq, because free nations do not threaten others or breed the ideologies of murder. By working for democracy, we serve the cause of peace."[8]

However, an argument based solely on mendicant patriarchalism diminishes the decision-making capabilities of Macapagal-Arroyo. As indicated by her decision to "spare" the life of Angelo de la Cruz (detailed in chapter 5), Macapagal-Arroyo is quite prepared to answer to an authority higher than the United States. Accordingly, I forward the argument that the Bush administration's rhetoric of humanitarianism conformed with Macapagal-Arroyo's Roman Catholic reading of the War on Terror. In particular, both presidents viewed their actions as conforming to God's will. Both pronounced that God *chose* them to lead their respective flocks in these "dark" times. To the extent that the political fundamentalism of Bush and Macapagal-Arroyo dovetailed, the Coalition of the Willing was a reality. When these moralities clashed, Macapagal-Arroyo departed from the path set forth by

Bush. In this chapter I consider the Philippines' Will to War. In the final chapter I consider the collapse of this "will."

THE FOREIGN POLICY OF MACAPAGAL-ARROYO

In her speech delivered on the 103rd Foundation Day of the Department of Foreign Affairs, on July 12, 2001, Macapagal-Arroyo noted that her father, as president, promoted the principle that Asian problems should be solved by Asian nations. Her father, though, also believed in cooperating with the United States because the two countries shared the common ideals of democracy, freedom, love for peace, and the rule of law. For herself, Macapagal-Arroyo forwarded eight policies, or realities, that she urged the department to advance. The first reality was that China, Japan, and the United States would retain a determining influence in the security situation and economic evolution of Asia. Macapagal-Arroyo spoke strongly for the "blossoming" of Philippine–U.S. relations that are "responsive to the new realities of globalization and the conjunction of democracy and the market." Her second reality was to situate Philippine foreign policy more firmly with the Association of South East Asian Nations (ASEAN). She said that it would be through the Philippines' commitment to ASEAN that the country would achieve global competitiveness toward attaining sustainable growth and development. Macapagal-Arroyo's third reality was to form stronger bilateral relations with Islamic countries, including Malaysia, Indonesia, Saudi Arabia, Pakistan, and others. A fourth reality was to promote greater multilateral and interregional cooperation within East Asia, while a fifth reality was to protect the national territory of the Philippines. This would be done through the broadening and deepening of bilateral relations with neighboring countries. The sixth and seventh realities addressed investment and tourism, respectively; combined, these addressed specific means of promoting economic growth and development within the country. Finally, Macapagal-Arroyo announced her eighth reality: the assertion that overseas Filipinos would continue to play a critical role in the country's economic and social stability.[9] As explained in chapter 2, the promotion of overseas employment has remained a centerpiece of Philippine economic planning for over three decades. The administration of Macapagal-Arroyo clearly has no indications of changing this reality.

The foreign policy of Macapagal-Arroyo, however, is also predicated on basic Catholic principles. As indicated in chapter 1, Macapagal-Arroyo has remained firm in her convictions to stress the government's adherence to Catholic dictums. Indeed, specific policies forwarded by Macapagal-Arroyo are deeply influenced by her religious beliefs, and in this way, she demonstrates a political fundamentalism similar to that of Bush. However, whereas Bush has used the War on Terror as a justification for preemptive strikes and military buildups, Macapagal-Arroyo has pursued a foreign policy underscored by a Catholic vision of peace. This vision generally consists of four elements: human rights, development, solidarity, and world order. Catholic teaching insists that peace is not the mere absence of war; instead, peace is the positive realization of the dignity of all humanity. According to this perspective, the objective becomes the recognition, respect, safeguarding, and promotion of the rights of people. Humanitarian intervention in international affairs is predicated on the belief that *the rights of persons take priority over the rights of states.* [10]

The second element of the Catholic understanding of peace is the notion of authentic development. This consists of three points: the right of all people to the means for their full development as human beings; the proposition that authentic human development consists of more than economic progress; and the affirmation that the affluent nations of the world have an obligation to share the benefits of development with the poor. [11] As discussed in the following, the reconstruction efforts of the Philippines fall squarely under the values expounded by authentic development. Through humanitarian intervention *after* the conflict, Filipinos were able to help uplift the Iraqi people as well as provide economic opportunities for Filipinos themselves.

Solidarity is the third element. In essence, this refers to an active commitment to the belief that we belong to one family under God. But more significant, especially with respect to foreign policy, solidarity consists of an attitude to communal efforts to bring about peace. [12] At the international level, this translates into a greater willingness to participate in multinational alliances, such as the Coalition of the Willing.

Last, the fourth element of world order focuses on the construction of world peace. This has, at times, been discordant with the justification for military intervention, particularly given the espousal of nonviolence. In practice, the Catholic vision of peace allows for a limited notion of war, encapsulated under the theory of "just war." [13]

By way of example, it is instructive to consider the strategies to confront terrorism as advocated by Bush and Macapagal-Arroyo. As explained in chapter 3, for Bush the War on Terror was an opportunity ordained by God, and it was his moral duty to lead the world's nations to a promised land free from evil. For Bush, accordingly, a particular conception of political reality was forwarded, one that emphasized binaries: good/evil, us/them, security/peril. This constituted an unbending form of thinking and language that parses people, institutions, behaviors, and ideologies into opposing camps. This sense of moral certitude forwarded by Bush and his administration was used to justify the use of preemptive strikes, military occupation, and the destruction of (alleged) terrorists and those countries that were said to harbor terrorists.[14] In his 2002 State of the Union address, Bush explained, "Our war against terror is only beginning." He said, "Thanks to the work of our law enforcement officials and coalition partners, hundreds of terrorists have been arrested." Bush continued, "My hope is that all nations will heed our call, and eliminate the terrorist parasites who threaten their countries and our own. Many nations are acting forcefully. . . . But some governments will be timid in the face of terror. And make no mistake about it: If they do not act, America will."[15]

Macapagal-Arroyo's approach to terrorism is more circumspect. Following the attacks of September 11, Macapagal-Arroyo developed a sixteen-point plan for the Philippines' counterterrorism program. Among these points, four are especially relevant for our present discussion. One point forwarded by Macapagal-Arroyo is to "pursue broader inter-faith dialogue to promote Christian and Muslim solidarity." Clearly reflecting a Catholic vision of peace, Macapagal-Arroyo explained, "Terrorists want to instigate a religious war. We must make this instead an opportunity to forge religious understanding, ecumenism and solidarity."[16]

A second point contradicts the dialogue-stunting discourse of Bush. Macapagal-Arroyo explained, "Nothing justifies terrorism but we must recognize the political, social and economic underpinnings of terrorism."[17] Rather that simply concede terrorism as resultant from an essentialized evil, Macapagal-Arroyo instead chooses to identify underlying causes, namely poverty. In a speech delivered at the International Institute for Strategic Studies in London, Macapagal-Arroyo explained, "We have put a face on terrorists, and now we must put a face on the poor. We will eliminate terrorism and we must eliminate poverty. If we do not, the breeding ground of resentment will begin again to plague another generation."[18] Similar to Bush, the Philippine president attributes certain terrorist acts to "resentment." However, unlike Bush's interpretation of terrorism, this one is not extrapolated from the terrorists' presumed blind jealousy but is based on a disparity between the "haves" and the "have-nots." Macapagal-Arroyo continued, "At the dawn of the 21st century, we cannot go another generation in the history of mankind without slaying the dragon of poverty. Leaders of all nations, rich and poor, must harness the power of modern society and technology to advance the quality of life of every global citizen." Accordingly, the Philippine president urged "the initiation of special community development programs in areas whose extreme poverty make them vulnerable to the courtship of terrorist groups." Whereas Bush was primarily concerned with the elimination of existing terrorist networks, Macapagal-Arroyo focused on eliminating the conditions that may foment the discontent manifest in acts of terror.[19]

A final point to be discussed is how Macapagal-Arroyo linked foreign policy with overseas employment. Macapagal-Arroyo claimed, "The interest of our overseas Filipino workers are paramount. The government is going out of its way to support their immediate transfer out of harm's way in the event of tactical contingencies anywhere in the world."[20] Speaking in acknowledgment of future conflicts related to the War on Terror, Macapagal-Arroyo stressed the necessity of protecting those living and working in other countries. This point, and many of her others, focused more on the humanitarian basis of terrorism and appeared to subsume state concerns with individual rights. From a perspective of political realism, this may seem discordant. And yet, predicated on a Catholic vision of peace, Macapagal-Arroyo is consistent in her moral foundations. Macapagal-Arroyo expressed her concern that "each and every Filipino has the responsibility to be aware and enlightened, to be vigilant and to act with discipline and with a genuine concern for the common good."[21] One need only compare this statement with that of Bush's conclusion to his 2002 State of the Union address: "Steadfast in our purpose, we now press on. We have known freedom's price. We have shown freedom's power. And in this great conflict, my fellow Americans, we will see freedom's victory."[22]

In short, the foreign policies of both Macapagal-Arroyo and Bush were predicated on a political fundamentalism. How this religiosity was manifest, however, accounts for the Philippines' Will to War and, as discussed in the next chapter, the Philippines' departure from the Coalition of the Willing.

JOINING THE COALITION

Hours after the September 11 attacks, Macapagal-Arroyo (along with other foreign dignitaries) dispatched a letter to Bush. Her sentiments would echo the religiosity that would typify the War on Terror. She began, "Nothing can describe the shock and horror of all humanity in the face of the unimaginable acts of terror inflicted on the United States today. All mankind is diminished by the extreme evil we saw unleashed on your cities." Macapagal-Arroyo offered the sympathies and services of the Filipino people. She explained that the Philippines would help in whatever way they could to strengthen the global effort to crush those responsible. In her conclusion, Macapagal-Arroyo said this was a dark day for all who abide by the basic kindness that makes communities possible and brotherhood a desirable condition.[23]

Macapagal-Arroyo clarified her support for the growing coalition during a speech delivered on September 27, 2001. On this occasion, Macapagal-Arroyo explained that the recently announced War on Terror was "a war where both persons and nations have to make a stand." She stated that it was a "war against barbarism of the most ruthless kind" and a "war against evil persons whose aim is to terrorize, to sow fear, to generate hatred." She affirmed, as did Bush, that it was "a war between good and evil." And similar to Bush, Macapagal-Arroyo forwarded a sense of urgency. She explained, "We must win, for the consequences of losing [would result in] a return to the dark ages when barbarians and wolves were at the gate."[24]

The initial discourse of Macapagal-Arroyo in this speech was one that resonated strongly with the discourse forwarded by the Bush administration. The civilized world was under attack from evil, and the consequences of inaction were dire indeed. However, at this point, Macapagal-Arroyo deviated from the Bush position. Macapagal-Arroyo implored her listeners to take care in the conduct of the war. She said, "In fighting this war, we must take care that we ourselves do not become barbarians."[25] As expressed in Romans 12:17, one must not repay evil for evil; rather, as written in Romans 12:20, "If thine enemy hunger, feed him; if he thirst, give him drink: for in so doing thou shalt heap coals of fire on his head." Macapagal-Arroyo is willing to participate in the War on Terror, but she appeared at this point to leave vengeance to the Lord.

Macapagal-Arroyo continued, "Without any loss of will and resolve, we will engage the enemies in battle using the institutions and instruments of freedom, of Christianity, and Islam." Macapagal-Arroyo then elaborated on her decision: "I decided to participate in this campaign because first, it is in our national interest; second, it is a moral cause; third, it is consistent with our constitution; and fourth, it is our obligation under the mutual defense treaty with the United States and under the United Nations." However, her next statement suggests that she perceived the War on Terror in terms that diverged from foreign policy considerations. She said, "Beyond formal treaties, there is in all of us a deep moral purpose that is more powerful than any legal instrument. It is our belief that evil must not be allowed to rule even an inch of this earth." Clearly, the political fundamentalism is as apparent in the rhetoric of Macapagal-Arroyo as it is in the rhetoric of Bush. However, Macapagal-Arroyo identified a different set of "specifics." Macapagal-Arroyo explicitly identified the aims of the United States: "President George W. Bush has defined its strategic objective: it is to eradicate terrorism everywhere and to extirpate it forever from the society of free, peace-loving peoples." Macapagal-Arroyo then stated simply that she supported this war aim. She agreed also to join the international counter-terrorist coalition and to work with the United Nations; she directed the relevant Philippine departments to make intelligence available for coalition members; she offered Philippine airspaces, airfields, and naval stations for transit and refueling; and she offered—if requested—noncombat troops, including medical, engineering, and support personnel, that could be deployed to battlefields if necessary. On the subject of armed forces participating in actual fighting, Macapagal-Arroyo was less firm. She stated, "Subject to the concurrence of the Philippine Congress, I am willing to provide combat troops if there is an international call for such troops." Simply put, if military troops were to be deployed, it would come at the request of the Philippine Congress and the international community; Macapagal-Arroyo would *not* be the person sending troops into harm's way.[26]

One could argue that Macapagal-Arroyo's decision—some would say reluctance—to send military personnel indicates trepidation on her part in the War on Terror. This interpretation, though, is unsatisfactory. Instead, I contend that the strategies forwarded by Macapagal-Arroyo are entirely consistent with her political fundamentalism. She concluded her London speech, for example, with the following statement:

> Victory in this struggle does not depend only on winning the battles of this war. We must also win the peace. And winning the peace means in the last analysis winning the battle for development. As Pope John Paul II says, "Development is the other name of peace." The peace and security we seek impels us to confront the conditions and also the reasons why terrorism can so easily spread. We know that evil causes terrorism but the evil of terrorism would not be able to spread so much if we did not have so much poverty. And so it is important to realize that terrorism thrives whenever there is poverty and misery.[27]

Simply put, Macapagal-Arroyo viewed the Coalition of the Willing as a means of combating poverty. As indicated earlier, Macapagal-Arroyo attempted to provide a material understanding to the act of terror. This stance was in opposition to the rhetoric of Bush that eliminated any possibility of discussion. And the understanding of terrorism, to Macapagal-Arroyo, was poverty. She explained, "The growth of terrorism is inextricably linked to the growth of mass poverty and, therefore, the eradication of terrorism will enable the sustained and effective alleviation of poverty. This is one of the reasons why we have committed to play a major role in the global war against terrorism." She emphasized, "The fingerlings of crime and terrorism may spawn in the waters of mass poverty. We must act on the two sides of the question."[28]

These themes were recurrent in subsequent months. On October 8, 2001, following the military intervention in Afghanistan, Macapagal-Arroyo reiterated the Philippine government's support of the U.S. action against terrorism. She indicated her support of the military action in Afghanistan and also vowed that the Philippines would be prepared "within its means, to work with the United Nations to assist the people of Afghanistan who have suffered much from hunger, deprivation and sickness for many years." She ended with a message to overseas Filipinos: "For Filipinos afar, in other places of the world—be with us in this fight, while we work together to keep you out of harm's way. Your government will be there to help you when you need to come home from perilous places."[29]

Macapagal-Arroyo, however, alternated between complete and unwavering support to a thinly veiled reticence. Leading up to the war in Iraq, for example, as the Bush administration was gathering momentum for military action, Macapagal-Arroyo continued to pray for peace. In a statement delivered on March 18, 2003, just two days before the start of the war, Macapagal-Arroyo said, "Up to this time, peace remains the best option. We keep our hopes high that the precarious situation can be resolved by a consensus of the international community; and I pray that Saddam Hussein will take all steps to avert war and pave the way for a peaceful resolution of the conflict."[30]

Even as combat operations began, Macapagal-Arroyo's support of the U.S.-led coalition was not based on a support for war per se. In a statement released on March 20, 2003, as the U.S.-led military strike on Iraq began, Macapagal-Arroyo announced, "We are part of the Coalition of the Willing in terms of political and moral support for actions to rid Iraq of weapons of mass destruction. We are part of a long-standing security alliance as well as the global coalition against terrorism." In this statement she immediately placed the Philippines' Will to War within the realities of regional alliances as well as within a long-standing support of the United States. She also argued that the Philippines' participation as a member of the coalition and its support of the invasion were necessary for the security and well-being of the Philippines: "This relationship is vital to our national security. It bears a significance to this war and to our combined efforts to fight terrorism in the Philippines and the region." She defined the attempt to rid Iraq of weapons of mass destruction as a "moral and political cause." Implicitly, Macapagal-Arroyo appeared to support the ends—the removal of weapons of mass destruction and so forth—but not the means. Pointedly, Macapagal-Arroyo affirmed, "We shall not deploy Philippine combat troops. But the Philippines is committed to extend peacekeeping and humanitarian assistance after the Iraq conflict."[31]

As combat operations neared an end, Macapagal-Arroyo issued a statement on April 9. She explained that as the war was virtually over, the coalition was now crossing the bridge between mopping up operations and beginning restoration. She continued, "We must remember that we have also benefitted in a significant way from this victory. We are now safer from weapons of mass destruction. We are more secure from the tentacles of worldwide terrorism abetted by rogue states. We have won freedom as much as the Iraqi people have won theirs."[32] Her statement thus replicated the *casus bellum* of the United States. Noticeably missing from her statements, however, was the vengeance that was more characteristic of members of the Bush administration.

Macapagal-Arroyo and her administration viewed the reconstruction of Iraq as serving two interrelated purposes. On one hand, it was presented as a humanitarian act. Foreign affairs secretary Blas Ople confirmed this purpose in his statement on the deployment of a humanitarian task force (detailed later). According to Ople, the sending of peacekeepers and migrant workers "are but natural extensions of the Philippines' policy of extending assistance to Iraq not in pursuit of the war but in 'building the peace.'"[33] On the other hand, the reconstruction contributed to resolving tensions in the southern Philippines and stabilizing relations in East Asia and Southeast Asia. Consequently, Macapagal-Arroyo remained firm in her resolve to support the coalition, as she viewed the Philippines' peacekeeping operations in Iraq as part and parcel of her domestic politics—namely, the elimination of poverty and the ongoing peace negotiations in the southern Philippines. Indeed, it is instructive to examine more closely the efforts of Macapagal-Arroyo to balance her support of the war against Iraq given the existence of Muslim separatist groups in her own country. In a statement released on April 16, 2003, Macapagal-Arroyo said, "We are now faced with the new battle to heal the wounds of war. Our humanitarian and peacekeeping mission to Iraq has a relevance to our own humanitarian and peacekeeping missions in Mindanao." She continued by explaining, "By helping our Muslim brethren in dire need halfway across the world, we deepen our awareness of the need to help our own suffering brethren in Mindanao. Forging ties with the Islamic world has been an integral part of our foreign policy and it helps us immeasurably in the cause of peace and development in Mindanao." Macapagal-Arroyo positioned the Philippines not as a participant in the war in Iraq but rather as a contributor to the reconstruction process. In this way, and by the fact that the Philippines did not contribute military troops during the invasion, Macapagal-Arroyo was able to legitimately claim that her policies are based solely on humanitarian efforts. *No one died as a result of Philippine foreign policy.* Macapagal-Arroyo further explained, "Our support for the restoration of democracy in Iraq . . . will have an important effect on the overall drive against terrorism in our country, as we demonstrate that extremism and evil can be transformed by the will of a people into humane self-governance." Downplaying the war itself, Macapagal-Arroyo presented a sanguine reading of the previous weeks of military action.[34]

Macapagal-Arroyo did not receive unanimous support in her decision to join—however limited—the Coalition of the Willing. Despite her efforts to the contrary, she was repeatedly accused by political opponents and critics in the media as being a "puppet" of the United States. Macapagal-Arroyo, indeed, attempted to counter this accusation in her statements of September 27, 2001. At that time the Philippine president explained, "Some say that we should not do the bidding of the United States. But this is a sovereign decision that is based only partly on our mutual defense treaty with the U.S. I committed the country to fight this fight because it is right."[35] Nevertheless, Macapagal-Arroyo was continually questioned for her motivations in supporting the Coalition of the Willing. To a large degree, criticism focused on the perceived "buying" of the Philippines' participation. In May 2003, for example, Macapagal-Arroyo undertook a state visit to the United States. In part, the purpose of her visit was to discuss plans for a postwar Iraq. Upon her arrival she was received with full military honors, and during a toast to the Philippine president, Bush said, "Our nations are natural partners. We are connected by an ocean, united by a shared history, and sustained by the bonds of family and culture."[36]

During this visit, the United States elevated the Philippines' status to a full-fledged partner in the war on terrorism; Bush disclosed plans to classify the country as a "major non-NATO ally." Such a designation would make it easier for the Philippine government to acquire military equipment. Later, in a joint press conference Bush declared, "The step will allow our countries to work together on military research and development and give the Philippines greater access to American defense equipment and supply." This status placed the Philippines on the same international level as Australia,

Egypt, and Israel, as far as military affairs were concerned. Of the designation, Macapagal-Arroyo remarked, "While Asia must take greater responsibility for its own political and economic security, it must also recognize that
strong relations with the U.S. will contribute greatly to regional peace and
prosperity, stability and security especially from terrorism."[37]

As part of initial arrangements, the United States would provide thirty
helicopters to the Armed Forces of the Philippines. At the time, the Philippine Air Force had only nine. Presidential chief of staff Rigoberto Tiglao
would explain, "This is very important symbolically and in substance, because acquiring helicopters is very difficult. You have to undergo a very te-
dious process."[38]

As alluded to earlier, the May 2003 agreements announced by Bush
and Macapagal-Arroyo were not unanimously supported by members of
the Philippine legislature. Senator Rodolfo Biazon, vice chairperson of
the Senate Committee on National Defense and Security, wondered what
the tradeoff would be with the United States elevating the Philippines'
military status. Explaining that it is impossible for a superpower such as
the United States to simply "give" a developing country anything, Senator Biazon concluded, "I am sure the tradeoff is much bigger than what
the U.S. has given us. But in fairness to President Bush, President Arroyo
can boast as soon as she returns that her trip was very fruitful."[39]

Relatedly, Senator Aquilino Pimentel Jr. expressed his concern that the
Philippines needed economic aid rather than military aid. Senator Pimentel
had been quite wary about the U.S. participation in the War on Terror and
especially of how America's actions would affect the Philippines. According
to Senator Pimentel, "President Bush must show that the U.S. can play
peace broker of the universe as it has done in the past, and to me this is the
best gift the U.S. can offer to the Filipino people, because if the U.S. suc-
ceeds, we will expect the influx of investors, both local and foreign."[40]

Other members of the Philippine Congress questioned the potential
role of the U. S. government in the internal affairs of the Philippines, especially with respect to potential separatist movements in the southern
Philippines. Representative Satur Ocampo acknowledged that "it seems an
affirmation that the Philippines is squarely behind the U.S." Accordingly, it
was inevitable, from the perspective of Representative Ocampo, that the
United States would interfere in the Philippines' internal conflict in Mindanao.[41]

Lastly, there were disagreements over the Philippines' course of action.
Senator Teresa Aquino-Oreta urged the government to not send a humanitarian mission to Iraq but instead to forward the money to an emergency fund

set up by ASEAN to fight the SARS (severe acute respiratory syndrome) virus. Alternatively, Senator Manuel Villar Jr. advised the Macapagal-Arroyo administration to suspend the operation pending a Senate inquiry into the government's financial capability to undertake the mission and to ensure legal and diplomatic protection for the force.[42]

REGIONAL ALLIANCES

From Macapagal-Arroyo's perspective, it was imperative that the Philippines not appear as a political puppet of the United States. As indicated in her eight realities of foreign policy, Macapagal-Arroyo sought to strengthen the position of the Philippines within various Southeast Asian and East Asian alliances. This was to be done through the pursuit of multilateral and bilateral agreements with neighboring countries in the areas of trade, investment, and other economic programs. Between 2001 and 2004 Macapagal-Arroyo undertook a number of visits throughout Asia, including the People's Republic of China, Hong Kong, Malaysia, and Brunei. In addition, she hosted a number of foreign dignitaries. The speeches and statements of Macapagal-Arroyo are telling in that she consistently linked terrorism with poverty and emphasized that the Coalition of the Willing could lead to greater solidarity among Asian nations. In early October 2001, for example, Prime Minister Thaksin Shinawatra of Thailand made a state visit to the Philippines. Macapagal-Arroyo thanked the prime minister for his support of the coalition and concluded, "As similar economies linked by a common ASEAN identity, I strongly believe in continuing to energize our partnership towards our shared goal of maintaining peace, ensuring stability and securing progress in ASEAN and the world at large."[43]

In October 2001, the Philippine president also delivered a keynote address before delegates of the Sixteenth East Asia Economic Summit in Hong Kong. On this occasion, just weeks after her strong support of the United States' emerging War on Terror, Macapagal-Arroyo clarified, "Our decision to join the American fight against terrorism was not an emotional one—it was a strategic decision. The fight against terrorism is a global fight—it touches each and every one of our nations and indeed we in the Philippines have first-hand experience."[44] This would not be the only occasion that Macapagal-Arroyo would indicate that the Philippines has long addressed issues of terrorism. Nor would this be the only time in which she referred to larger objectives within the War on Terror. As discussed, Macapagal-Arroyo's agreement to participate as a coalition member was determined mostly by her belief that through international partnerships other problems could be resolved—namely, poverty. Crucially, though, Macapagal-Arroyo was compelled to balance her support of the Coalition of the Willing within a political environment that largely distrusted the efforts of the U.S.-led War on Terror.

In January 2003, as the United States continued to press for war, Iraq's UN ambassador, Mohammed Aldouri, warned that Muslims around the world would attack American facilities if the United States invaded his country. In response, Macapagal-Arroyo indicated that it was too early and premature for the Philippines to take a stand on the crisis. She said that her main concern was the safety and welfare of the estimated 1.4 million Filipinos working in the Middle East. She continued to appeal to Iraq, however, to fully cooperate with the U.S. resolution for the sake of world peace.[43]

In late October 2003, Macapagal-Arroyo traveled to Malaysia to attend the Tenth Session of the Islamic Summit Conference of the Organization of Islamic Conference (OIC). Established in 1969 in response to a call for Islamic solidarity by the late Saudi Arabian king Faisal Ibn Abdulaziz, the OIC currently has fifty-seven member states. The stated goal of the OIC is not religious, however, but rather to strengthen the solidarity and cooperation among Islamic states in various political, economic, social, cultural, and scientific endeavors. Its basic aims are to promote international peace and security founded on the basis of justice; to protect holy places of Islam; and to support the struggles of Palestinian peoples. The attendance of Macapagal-Arroyo was historic, as it marked the first time in the thirty-four-year history of the OIC that a Philippine president had been invited to attend. Symbolically and materially, Macapagal-Arroyo's visit was vitally important to the ongoing peace process of the southern Philippines, the establishment of regional alliances with neighboring Asian states, and as a sign of Asian solidarity.

The regional alliances fostered by Macapagal-Arroyo were, in short, a basic component of her overall foreign policy because of domestic concerns—namely, the importance of Malaysia and Indonesia in facilitating a peaceful resolve to the conflict in the southern Philippines. Accordingly, Macapagal-Arroyo has been concerned with maintaining stable relations with her neighboring countries. However, to the extent that these countries have been less than favorable to the United States' policies toward the Middle East, Macapagal-Arroyo has had to walk a very thin line. In so doing, Macapagal-Arroyo consistently portrayed the Philippines' presence in Iraq as one of humanitarian assistance, of providing jobs for Filipinos (and thus contributing to overall development of the country), and of providing assistance to the Iraqis.

ORDERING JOBS

During her speech of January 28, 2002, delivered at the International Institute for Strategic Studies, Macapagal-Arroyo said, "A new kind of war requires a new kind of peace. The hallmarks of any new global alliance to alleviate poverty must be market-driven, solve a real human problem, and demand accountability from those nations that benefit."[46] Thus, in an interesting mix of Catholicism and neoliberalism, Macapagal-Arroyo viewed the War on Terror as an opportunity to confront poverty. Overseas employment as foreign policy would thus eliminate two interrelated problems: poverty and, by extension, terrorism. This could be accomplished through the peaceful promotion of development through solidarity and humanitarian intervention.

On April 14, 2003, as Pentagon officials declared a cessation of major combat operations in Iraq, President Macapagal-Arroyo signed Executive Orders 194 and 195. Through the first order, the president approved the formation of a public–private sector task force to coordinate Philippine participation in the postwar reconstruction of Iraq. Specifically, EO-194 codified the establishment of the Public–Private Sector Task Force on the Reconstruction and Development of Iraq (hereafter referred to as the Task Force). Operationally, the Task Force was assigned the dual purpose of assisting "the participation of Philippine companies in the rehabilitation and development of the Iraqi infrastructure" and developing "procedures to expedite deployment of Philippine manpower and other services in the fulfillment of contracts." This conformed readily with the earlier strategies enacted by the Philippine Overseas Employment Administration to increase the efficiency in the deployment of contract workers and to meet the larger goal of deploying "one million" workers annually.

The Task Force would function to market Philippine contractors, migrant workers, and service providers with foreign firms as subcontractors for projects related to the reconstruction of Iraq. In this manner, the Task Force was to facilitate the arrangement of subcontracts for Filipino construction workers in a process mirroring that established in the 1970s. Specifically, the Task Force was to do the following: provide representation on behalf of the Philippine government and the private sector with national, multilateral agencies, and international private contractors involved in the reconstruction of Iraq; serve as a one-stop hub linking Philippine subcontractors with their primary contractors and major subcontractors; identify and qualify Philippine-based companies and other entities to ensure that service standards were competitive and of the highest quality; and develop procedures and review workers and labor service–oriented qualifications in Iraq with the Philippines Overseas Employment Administration to expedite deployment.[47]

The Task Force, exhibiting consonance and continuity with the Macapagal-Arroyo administration's overall philosophy toward overseas employment, was to maximize efficiency and rapidity in the deployment of workers. This translated into efforts to remove administrative red tape and present the most attractive overall labor-export package to foreign contractors. In its marketing efforts, the Task Force stressed that the Philippines had the world's largest pool of skilled labor available for immediate international mobilization; that Philippine companies and workers are among the most experienced in the world, particularly in infrastructure and development; that the country has the full range of expertise and capabilities needed in reconstruction projects such as those presently found in Iraq; that Filipino workers have long been in demand among primary contractors, as they have a well-earned reputation worldwide for their quality, productivity, work ethic, social skills, and English-speaking skills; and, finally, that over 150 selected and accredited companies are readily available.

EO-194 begins with the assertion that the Philippines, as a member of the United Nations, desires to contribute to both the immediate humanitarian needs of the Iraqi people and the multinational effort for the long-term reconstruction and development of Iraq. Discursively, the Philippine government is establishing that it is not "going it alone" but rather is affiliated with a larger, multinational effort. Significantly, Macapagal-Arroyo declared that the Philippines "will help in [its] own limited way in this struggle of the Iraqi people by sending Filipinos across the seas to clasp hands with the victims of war." This statement is telling in that it relates directly to the second element of the Catholic vision of peace—namely, that the relatively affluent nations have an obligation to share the benefits of development with the poor.

Former foreign affairs secretary Roberto Romulo, chair of the newly created Task Force, explained, "The Philippines is extending humanitarian assistance to Iraq to the extent that our modern national budget will permit." He indicated that the Philippines was helping extensively in the work of reconstruction and rehabilitation through the Philippines' "greatest asset"—its "skilled labor force." Romulo also drew on a stock positioning of the Philippines as a humanitarian country, one that, although limited in resources, is willing to provide its only viable resource: human labor. Romulo continued, "We are fortunate and we should all be thankful that the lives of our [overseas Filipino workers] in the Middle East are safe as a result of the decisive action in Iraq. Now we can turn quickly to doing what we do best: providing the best-skilled and most mobile labor force in the world to help rebuild Iraq."[48] By framing the war in these terms, Romulo provided further justification for the U.S.-led military intervention in Iraq; namely, it was the decisive action initiated by Bush that protected the thousands of vulnerable Filipino contract workers deployed throughout the Middle East. But Romulo also framed the Philippines as being able to take an equally decisive and positive step: the provision of labor.

Despite these statements, there is no doubt that the Philippines utilized its position as a member of the Coalition of the Willing to support its efforts to participate in the reconstruction of Iraq. Moreover, this opportunity was anticipated well in advance. In March 2003, Ambassador Roy Cimatu, head of the Middle East Preparedness Team, explained in a teleconference with Macapagal-Arroyo that a total of fifty thousand to one hundred thousand jobs would be available in the rebuilding of Iraq and that Filipino workers would be in high demand in Iraq and Kuwait. Jobs would be readily forthcoming once Iraq was cleared of explosives, mines, and military installations. Macapagal-Arroyo acknowledged that jobs for Filipinos after the war were one of the benefits the country would reap from joining the U.S.-led Coalition of the Willing.[49]

Months before the invasion, Philippine officials expressed concern over the safety and welfare of Filipino workers. Indeed, contingency plans for evacuation procedures were implemented to provide help for the estimated 1.4 million Filipinos who were deployed throughout the Middle East. Macapagal-Arroyo was consistent in her positioning of transnational migrants. In the course of the war, she "directed the Department of Foreign Affairs to take the necessary measures together with the Middle East Preparedness Team to ensure the safety of [Philippine] nationals and at the same time, preserve diplomatic normalcy as much as possible." She assured "all Filipino families and their loved ones that [the] government will take care of [its] overseas Filipinos."[50] This is not to say that all members of the Philippine government viewed the presence of overseas Filipinos in the Middle East as threatened. Nicon Fameronag, a member of the Middle East Preparedness Team, for example, discounted the possibility of Filipinos being repatriated if fighting broke out. According to Fameronag, most of the conflict would take place in Iraq, and the majority of Filipinos were in other parts of the Middle East and thus out of harm's way. Nevertheless, labor secretary Patricia Sto. Tomas said that various ambassadors, as well as labor officials in Lebanon, Bahrain, and Syria, were regularly checking on the condition of overseas Filipino workers.[51]

By far, the bulk of preparations centered on the acquisition of contracts. Early in 2003, before the onset of military operations, the U.S. government identified fourteen American firms that were to be considered for contracts for the rebuilding of a postwar Iraq. Indeed, it was reported that the Bush administration launched the bidding process for reconstruction efforts in mid-February, a month before the invasion began and at a time when the United Nations was still trying to come up with a compromise to avert war.[52] As reported in *The Guardian*, even as the United Nations was trying to avert war, the U.S. government was actually *awarding* construction contracts to rebuild Iraq. Halliburton, once headed by U.S. vice president Dick Cheney, had already been awarded a contract to resurrect the Iraqi oilfields following war. Other companies included Bechtel Corporation, Kellogg, Brown and Root, Stevedoring Services of America, and the Fluor Corporation. Many of these corporations had long histories of hiring Filipino contract workers. Indeed, many participated in the rebuilding of the 1991 Gulf War. Most recently, Halliburton had hired Filipino (and Asian Indian) workers to construct the detention facilities for "terrorists" detained at Guantanamo Bay, Cuba. The rush was on. Billions of dollars were to be made in Iraq, and numerous governments were ready to take advantage. According to one industry executive, "It's a sensitive topic because we still haven't gone to war." However, the executive conceded, "These companies are really in a position to win something out of this geopolitical situation."[53]

The conclusion of the war, however, saw an intensive effort on behalf of the Philippine state to secure employment contracts. In May, for example, Macapagal-Arroyo used her state visit to the United States in part to help market Philippine labor. During Macapagal-Arroyo's state visit, she met with top American contractors to ensure that the Philippines would share in the postwar reconstruction projects. Romulo said of the president's mission, "The task force needs to continue to aggressively market and prepare companies and workers for deployment."[54]

Romulo acknowledged also that US$2.4 billion had already been allocated by the U.S. Congress for the rebuilding efforts; some estimates placed the total cost as high as US$100 billion over a five-year span. Romulo also clarified that Philippine officials were hoping to capitalize on public workers and energy industry projects, as well as other noncore activities, such as information technologies, finance and accounting, catering, and logistics. Romulo added that "it's not just a question of sending people, because there is scope to do a certain amount of back-processing here." In other words, Romulo intimated that employment opportunities in the Philippines may also be forthcoming in the postwar effort. As a case in point, he noted that Flor Daniel, one of the fourteen firms set to participate in the reconstruction of Iraq, already had employed about eight hundred Filipino engineers doing designs for overseas projects.[55]

The Task Force perceived Kuwait to be a key entry point for reconstruction efforts in Iraq. During May 2003, the Task Force sent a seven-person delegation to Kuwait, meeting with key officials of the Kuwaiti business chamber. Romulo indicated that "Kuwait has a long history of commercial and cultural relations with Iraq and is poised to be the main jump-off point." He continued, "Clearly the Kuwaitis have a leg up on everybody else and are going in there; and in our various meetings they expressed their eagerness to do this in partnership with Philippine companies. They said they have the capital and the knowledge of the market and we have the skilled labor."[56] Expressing a long-held view that the comparative advantage of the Philippines is labor, Romulo and other members of the Task Force continually stressed the advantages of partnerships with both the United States and Kuwait.

Jun Campillo, spokesperson for the Task Force, indicated that they would offer services as subcontractors to British and U.S. firms based in either Kuwait or Iraq. In a radio interview, Campillo acknowledged that the Philippines, along with other countries of the Coalition of the Willing, were "positioning and trying to get contracts for their countrymen." Campillo explained further that, during the 1980s, the Philippines had as many as thirty thousand workers in Iraq and that the Task Force hoped to exceed this figure. Earlier in the month, Ople indicated that the Philippines could possibly garner one hundred thousand jobs in the reconstruction effort.[57]

Also in May, the Philippine Overseas Employment Administration (POEA) distributed an advisory to clarify employment opportunities in the reconstruction efforts in Iraq. It indicated that, as of the date of publication (May 15, 2003), there had been no requests for labor or job orders from foreign principals or contractors; however, these were expected. The Task Force, though, was exerting efforts toward acquiring a considerable share of all business and employment opportunities. Initial projections, according to the POEA, were on the order of two thousand and three thousand job requests within the first two years of the reconstruction. The advisory also specified the role of the POEA. This would be a "promotional and facilitative role insofar as manpower-related matters [were] concerned." Moreover, the POEA would "produce a list of qualified local service contractors and local recruitment agencies for the manpower-sourcing reference of prime contractors." The POEA would also "formulate recruitment and hiring guidelines to facilitate deployment."[58] These guidelines were specified the following month with the release of a memorandum.[59]

In July, the Task Force met with over one hundred public- and private-sector participants for a briefing on the Postwar Iraq Reconstruction Program. Speakers included Bruce Derrick, country representative of KBR Halliburton-Philippines, and Wendy Chamberlain, ambassador and USAID assistant administrator for Asia and the Near East. Philippine representatives included administrators of the POEA, National Labor Relations Commission, and the Department of Foreign Affairs. At the meeting, labor undersecretary Manuel Imson presented an overview of the rules, programs, and services offered by the Department of Labor and Employment (DOLE) for the deployment of overseas workers. He specified the following measures, which, as recalled from chapter 2, exhibit continuity with a neoliberal approach for maximum efficiency. First, it would provide a listing and profiling of licensed agencies and contractors; second, it would make available the quick processing of migrant workers to Iraq through the "one-stop processing" center at the POEA (this would ensure that deployment schedules would be met by recruitment agencies and contractors); third, its labor attachés would conduct on-site project verifications; fourth, the DOLE's Technical Education and Skills Development Authority would train and certify Iraq-bound workers; and, fifth, DOLE would provide orientation on assistance programs for workers. In conclusion, Imson urged participants to use the DOLE's Computerized National Manpower Registry System (CN-MRS), a database of workers' skills and competencies; approximately 1.2 million Filipinos were in the registry. Imson added, "We have also opened in the CNMRS a special category for skilled Muslim workers in the southern Philippines."[60]

Later in the year, during October, representatives of the Philippines attended the International Donor's Conference for Iraq, held in Madrid, Spain. Over three hundred private-sector companies were in attendance, representing over seventy countries. Ali Allawi, interim trade minister of the U.S.-installed Iraqi Governing Council said, "The new Iraq will be above all a market-oriented economy. We expect and fully hope to achieve a stable, democratic, modern and progressive country in the very near future with the assistance of the international community and the assistance of the international private sector." He continued, "No sector of the economy will be closed to foreign investment with the exception of the oil sector."[61] It was presumed that the United States would mostly control the oil industry. However, the remainder of the country was completely open for business. Thirty-eight countries pledged loans and grants totaling approximately US$35.9 billion (excluding humanitarian assistance, export credits, and guarantees). The remaining thirty-five countries were "scouting" for economic opportunities, lacked resources to make presence, or were unable to pledge donations. The Philippines made no pledge of monetary assistance.

In its deployment of migrant workers, the Philippine government was concerned with competition from Iraqi workers, a concern that was discordant with the rhetoric of humanitarian intervention. In the aftermath of the war, underemployment and unemployment in Iraq were estimated to be at about 50 percent of the labor force. This figure, moreover, did not include the half-million Iraqi refugees nor the quarter-million internal refugees that were displaced by the conflict. American and other foreign contractors, consequently, would face considerable pressure to hire Iraqi workers. Officials for the Philippines ascertained, however, that foreign companies were reluctant to hire Iraqis. On one hand, Iraqis were perceived as untrustworthy—their country was, after all, invaded, even if under the pretext of liberation—and, on the other hand, companies would prefer to hire from labor-exporting countries that they had worked with in the past. It was on this basis, especially, that members of the Task Force felt confident. On May 28, 2003, Romulo explained, "We have names of 1 million workers, from skilled mechanical engineers to crane operators, who have passports and are ready to go. Priority for jobs will go to Iraqis. We have to bear in mind that there are 6 million unemployment Iraqis, and they are known for their work ethic. But when it comes to skilled labor, we definitely have the value-added."[62]

The Philippines, as a member of the Coalition of Opportunists, was not alone in its attempt to capitalize on the reconstruction efforts. Indeed, Romulo warned, "We have to act quickly to establish our role because there are about 50 members of the coalition and most are angling for a piece of the action." He continued, "The best opportunity is for experienced Philippine companies and skilled workers because the primary contractors have first-hand experience with Philippine companies and skilled labor." Romulo also indicated that U.S. firms would be outsourcing up to 70 percent of all labor needs, preferably to countries that were part of the Coalition of the Willing.[63]

KEEPING THE PEACE

As part of the Philippines' participation as a member of the Coalition of the Willing, the government prepared to deploy a small contingent of peacekeeping forces. To this end, Executive Order 195 created an additional task force to provide humanitarian assistance to Iraq. Initially, the Philippine government agreed to send a humanitarian contingent of approximately five hundred personnel—mostly military engineers, police, doctors, nurses, and social workers—to Iraq, at cost of six hundred million Philippine pesos. Presidential spokesperson Ignacio Bunye said, "[The humanitarian force] will play a key role in restoring order and normalcy [in Iraq]. The present chaos in the streets is a normal byproduct of a sudden power vacuum which our peacekeepers, together with those from other nations, can help fill. Our doctors and nurses can help both in medical treatment and in promoting public health."[64] This peacekeeping force, however, was quickly scaled down when the government learned that the United States would not foot the bill for the force's deployment. The presence of this peacekeeping force in Iraq, however, was deemed to be crucial so that the Philippines would be seen as a loyal member of the Coalition of the Willing. As indicated, the Philippine government was not the only country that attempted to garner a labor niche in war-torn Iraq. A general consensus was that *any* semblance of support for the United States might translate into lucrative contracts.

According to Ople, though, the deployment was a "voluntary" response to requests from the U.S.-led coalition to contribute to the rebuilding efforts of Iraq. He clarified, "There will be no combat role for the Philippine forces. They will not be deployed in danger areas. They will be deployed in contiguous areas which means that they will function as a unit rather than as separate, disparate groups." Ople added that this was not out of the ordinary for the Philippines; indeed, peacekeeping forces had been deployed to Cambodia, Kosovo, and East Timor. He concluded, "This is not the time to retreat into our shell and ignore the realities of history being played out in the Middle East, especially in Iraq."[65] Discursively, the Philippine government forwarded two seemingly disparate positions. On one hand, the president, along with certain other officials, continued to forward a humanitarian position, one that certainly gave lip service to the welfare of the Iraqi peoples. Macapagal-Arroyo likewise viewed the deployment of peacekeeping forces as conducive to the ongoing peace negotiations in the southern Philippines. On the other hand, the Task Force consistently forwarded a neoliberal position, one that stressed the comparative advantage of the Philippines. The Iraqis were seen not so much as oppressed or exploited peoples needing assistance as they were competitors in the rebuilding process. The deployment of peacekeeping forces was thus a small price to pay for access to bigger contracts. This bifurcated policy approach to the reconstruction of Iraq contributed to the ambiguities surrounding the Philippine government during the months to come.

THE THREATS TO RECONSTRUCTION

Since April 2003, the Philippine Task Force worked aggressively to secure contracts and subcontracts through both U.S. and Kuwaiti firms. Deployment, however, was hampered by the increasingly dangerous situation. Within days of the "liberation" of Iraq, rebel forces began targeting foreigners—in Iraq and neighboring countries—in an attempt to pressure members of the coalition to leave Iraq. These efforts included suicide and other forms of bombings, kidnappings, and shootings. On May 12, 2003, for example, suicide bombers targeted a residential complex in Riyadh, Saudi Arabia. The complex was occupied by Americans and other Westerners working on construction and defense contracts with the Saudi government. At least ten people died, with over sixty others injured. Among the dead were three Filipino workers: Serafin Hernandez and Getulio Templo, both of whom worked for Vinnell Arabia, a subsidiary of the U.S.-based Northrop Grumman Corporation; and Rogelio Pababero, who was a plant operator at Al Jadewell Water Treatment Camp.[66]

In response to the Riyadh bombings, foreign affairs spokesperson Victoriano Lecaros said that the Philippine government had no plans to pull out its nonessential staff from its foreign mission in Saudi Arabia, despite an order by the U.S. government to remove part of its personnel. Lecaros indicated that Filipino workers were not the intended targets of the attacks so it was not necessary for the Philippines to remove its personnel. Likewise, labor secretary Patricia Sto. Tomas said that the Philippines would continue to deploy migrant workers to Saudi Arabia. She said that there was no need to ban workers from deployment to the country since it would not help or normalize the situation.[67]

Later that year, in October, five bombings in Baghdad killed over forty people and wounded over two hundred. Macapagal-Arroyo indicated in a statement released by the Office of the President, "This series of atrocities will not discourage us from sending medical and peacekeeping troops to a nation that is indeed in dire need of help." Presidential spokesperson Ignacio Bunye explained further, "The latest series of attacks constitutes an assault against the international solidarity for peace, democracy and freedom. The Philippines joins the international community in condemning them."[68] He added, "It is sad that the restoration of freedom to the Iraqi people continues to be hobbled by uncertainty, but we are not intimidated in the least. Our commitment remains firm and we will not relent until peace and security is achieved in Iraq."[69]

Attacks continued. In April 2004, a Filipino truck driver was kidnapped, along with eight other workers from Pakistan, Turkey, Nepal, India, and Iran. Even though all were released, the incident compelled the Macapagal-Arroyo administration to reconsider the Philippines' presence in Iraq. The government's Cabinet Overnight Committee on Internal Security was said to be reassessing the situation and calibrating its options of whether to pull the Filipino contingent out of Iraq. Macapagal-Arroyo indicated, "I would like to assure [the nation] that the safety and security of our nationals are on top of the government agenda and that close monitoring is in place."[70] One month later, however, Rodrigo Reyes, another Filipino truck driver, was killed with two Ukrainian companions when their convoy was ambushed in Iraq. Vice President Teofisto Guingona Jr. said of the incident that the Philippines had done its part, "signaling to the world" that it supports the United States' "so-called war on terror," but stressed, "Now is the time to review the reasons why our troops are in Iraq." Macapagal-Arroyo at this point was less committed, saying "This incident does not call for the mass evacuation of our workers, although we are prepared for a calibrated response to any emergent contingencies." She did, though, promise to withdraw the peacekeeping contingent as well as order the relocation or evacuation of the migrant workers if the situation worsened.[71]

Efforts to participate in the reconstruction program were, however, limited by these attacks. As early as July 13, Philippine ambassador Jose Ibazeta, special envoy to the Middle East, said, "None of the reconstruction requiring Filipino labor and expertise can be undertaken until security has stabilized." He acknowledged also that Philippine Embassy official in Baghdad had reported to the Department of Foreign Affairs that Iraqis planned to target any foreigner identified with the coalition forces.[72] In August 2003, the POEA issued an advisory indicating, "Philippine engineering and construction firms, recruitment agencies and Filipino workers would have to wait for at least one more year before they [could] get labor contracts in the post-war reconstruction of Iraq. The Philippine government would not allow the deployment of Filipino workers to Iraq until the security situation in the country [had] normalized."[73] This statement was a far cry from the expected one hundred thousand jobs awaiting Filipinos. But it also indicates a change in the Macapagal-Arroyo administration. This change, moreover, appears to stem more so from Macapagal-Arroyo herself than it does to members of the Task Force. Although Macapagal-Arroyo remained firm in her commitment of maintaining peacekeepers in the region, she appears to have reconsidered the massive deployment of workers to Iraq sometime following the death of Reyes. In early May, the president suspended the sending of Filipino workers to Iraq.[74] In a little more than two months, the situation would worsen.

NOTES

1. Office of the Press Secretary, "Joint Statement between the U.S. and the Philippines," November 20, 2001, www.whitehouse.gov/news/releases/2001/11/20011120-13.html (March 31, 2004).

2. Office of the Press Secretary, "U.S. and the Philippines."

3. Office of the Press Secretary, "Remarks by President Bush and President Arroyo in a Photo Opportunity," October 18, 2003, www.whitehouse.gov/news/releases/2003/10/20031018-11.html (March 31, 2004).

4. Office of the Press Secretary, "Remarks by Bush and Arroyo."

5. Office of the Press Secretary, "Remarks by the President to the Philippine Congress," October 18, 2003, www.whitehouse.gov/news/releases/2003/10/20031018-12.html (March 31, 2004).

6. Anthony Woodiwiss, *Globalisation, Human Rights, and Labour Law in Pacific Asia* (Cambridge: Cambridge University Press, 1998), 102. See also Stanley Karnow, *In Our Image: America's Empire in the Philippines* (New York: Random House, 1989).

7. Office of the Press Secretary, "President to the Philippine Congress."

8. Office of the Press Secretary, "President to the Philippine Congress."

9. Office of the President, "PGMA's Speech during the 103rd Foundation Day of the Department of Foreign Affairs," July 12, 2001, www.opnet.ops.gov.ph/speech-2001july12.htm (August 9, 2004).

10. United States Institute of Peace (USIP), "Special Report 69: Catholic Contributions to International Peace," April 9, 2001, www.usip.org/pubs/specialreports/sr69.html (August 9, 2004).

11. USIP, "Special Report 69."

12. USIP, "Special Report 69."

13. USIP, "Special Report 69."

14. David Domke, *God Willing? Political Fundamentalism in the White House, the "War on Terror," and the Echoing Press* (London: Pluto Press, 2004), 25.

15. Office of the Press Secretary, "President Delivers [2002] State of the Union Address," January 29, 2002, www.whitehouse.gov/releases/2002/01/20020129-11.html (April 12, 2004).

16. Office of the President, "PGMA's Speech during the Command Conference on Anti-Terrorism," March 27, 2003, www.op.gov.ph/speeches/ (July 26, 2004).

17. Office of the President, "Anti-Terrorism."

18. Department of Foreign Affairs (DFA), "PGMA's Speech during a Lecture at the International Institute for Strategic Studies (IISS)," January 28, 2002, www.dfa.gov.ph/archive/speech/gma/iiss.htm (August 18, 2004).

19. DFA, "IISS Lecture."

20. Office of the President, "Anti-Terrorism."

21. Office of the President, "Anti-Terrorism."

22. Office of the Press Secretary, "2002 State of Union Address."

23. Office of the President, "PGMA's Letter to U.S. President George W. Bush regarding Terrorist Attack in the U.S.A.," September 12, 2001, www.opnet.ops.gov.ph/speech2001sept12a.htm (August 9, 2004).

24. Office of the President, "PGMA's Speech during a Dinner with the Foreign Correspondents of the Philippines (FOCAP)," September 27, 2001, www.opnet.ops.gov.ph/speech-2001sept27.htm (August 18, 2004).

25. Office of the President, "FOCAP Speech."

26. Office of the President, "FOCAP Speech."

27. DFA, "IISS Lecture."

28. Office of the President, "PGMA's Arrival Statement Coming from Beijing China," October 31, 2001, www.opnet.ops.gov.ph/speech-2001Oct31.htm (August 19, 2004).

29. Office of the President, "PGMA's Message Reiterating the Philippine Government Support on the U.S. Action against Terrorism," October 8, 2001, www.opnet.ops.gov.ph/speech-2001oct31.htm (August 9, 2004).

30. Office of the President, "PGMA's Statement on Our Preparedness re the Iraq Situation," March 18, 2003, www.ops.gov.ph/speeches2003/speech-2003mar18.htm (August 9, 2004).

31. Office of the President, "PGMA's Statement on the Military Strike Initiated by the United States and Its Coalition Partners against Iraq," March 20, 2003, www.ops.gov.ph/speeches2003/speech-2003mar20a.htm (August 9, 2004).

32. Office of the President, "PGMA's Statement on Iraq War," April 9, 2003, www.ops.gov.ph/speeches2003/speech-2003apr09.htm (August 9, 2004).

33. Department of Foreign Affairs, "Ople Convenes R. P. Humanitarian Task Force to Iraq," April 22, 2003, www.dfa.gov.ph/news/pr/pr2003/apr/pr184.htm (August 29, 2003).

34. Office of the President, "PGMA's Statement on the Mission to Iraq," April 16, 2003, www.ops.gov.ph/speeches/2003/speech-2003apr16.htm (October 15, 2003).

35. Office of the President, "FOCAP Speech."

36. Associated Free Press, "GMA Accorded Lavish Banquet at White House," *Manila Times*, May 21, 2003, www.manilatimes.net/national/2003/may/21/top_stories/20030521top2.html (March 26, 2004).

37. Ma. Theresa Torres, "Bush OK's Stronger RP-US Military Ties," *Manila Times*, May 21, 2003, www.manilatimes.net/national/2003/may/21/top_stories/20030521top1.html (March 26, 2004).

38. Torres, "Stronger RP-US Ties."

39. Torres, "Stronger RP-US Ties."

40. Torres, "Stronger RP-US Ties."

41. Torres, "Stronger RP-US Ties."

42. "RP to Seek 30,000 Jobs in Iraq for Pinoys," May 1, 2003, *Philippine Star*, www.philstar.com/philstar/ (November 14, 2003).

43. Office of the President, "PGMA's Speech during a Dinner in Honor of Prime Minister Thaksin Shinawatra of the Kingdom of Thailand," October 12, 2001, www.opnet.ops.gov.ph/speech-2001oct12.htm (August 19, 2004).

44. Office of the President, "PGMA's Keynote Address before the Delegates of the 16th East Asia Economic Summit," October 29, 2001, www.opnet.ops.gov.ph/speech-2001oct29.htm (August 19, 2004).

45. Ma. Theresa Torres, "Iraq's UN Envoy Warns of Muslim Attacks on US Interests If War Erupts," January 21, 2003, *Manila Times*, www.manilatimes.net/national/2003/jan/31/top_stories/20020131top4.html (March 26, 2004).

46. DFA, "IISS Speech."

47. This information is provided by the Philippine Task Force for the Reconstruction of Iraq's website, www.engagephilippines.com (August 4, 2004).

48. Office of the President, "Task Force to Secure Organize RP Role in Iraq Reconstruction," April 20, 2003, www.news.ops.gov.ph/archives2003/apr20.htm (August 29, 2003).

49. Ma. Theresa Torres, "100,000 Jobs Await Pinoys in Postwar Iraq," *Manila Times*, March 28, 2003, www.manilatimes.net/national/2003/mar/28/top_stories/20030328top2.html (April 9, 2004).

50. Office of the President, "Preparedness re Iraq."

51. Torres, "100,000 Jobs Await."

52. "Iraq: Reconstruction and U.S. Interest," *Globe and Mail*, April 1, 2003, accessed through CorpWatch, www.corpwatch.org/news/PND.jsp?articleid=6228 (November 14, 2003).

53. Danny Penman, "USA: Firms Set for Postwar Contracts," *Guardian*, March 11, 2003, www.corpwatch.org/news/PND.jsp?articleid=5928 (November 14, 2003).

54. Gil Cabacungan, "President to Meet US Contractors during Visit," *Inquirer News Service*, May 1, 2003, www.inq7.net/brk/2003/may/01/text/brkofw_1-1-p.htm (November 14, 2003).

55. Pia Lee-Brago, "RP to Gain from 14 US Firms Awarded Contracts to Rebuild Iraq," *Philippine Star*, May 5, 2003, www.philstar.com/philstar (November 14, 2003).

56. Mayen Jaymalin, "Kuwaitis Partnering with RP in Iraq Rebuilding Drive," *Philippine Star*, May 12, 2003, www.philstar.com/philstar (November 14, 2003).

57. "RP to Seek 30,000 Jobs in Iraq for Pinoys," *Philippine Star*, May 1, 2003, www.philstar.com/philstar/ (November 14, 2003).

58. Philippine Overseas Employment Administration, "Advisory No. 4, Series of 2003," May 15, 2003, www.poea.gov.ph/html/iraq.html (September 11, 2003).

59. Philippine Overseas Employment Administration, "Memorandum Circular No. 16, Series of 2003," June 11, 2003, www.poea.gov/ph/html/iraq.html (September 11, 2003).

60. Department of Labor and Employment, "RP to Ensure Deployment of Skilled Workers to Iraq," July 16, 2003, www.dole.gov.ph/news/pressreleases2003/July/203.htm (November 14, 2003).

61. Associated Free Press, "Iraq Tells Investors It's Open for Business," *Manila Times*, October 24, 2003, www.manilatimes.net/national/2003/oct/24/business/20031024bus8.html (April 9, 2004).

62. Patricia O'Connell, "A Philippine Foothold in Iraq," *Business Week Online*, appearing on Philippine Task Force for the Reconstruction of Iraq's website on May 28, 2003, www.engagephilippines.com/news/foothold_iraq.html (August 29, 2003).

63. Lee-Brago, "RP to Gain."

64. Ma. Theresa Torres, "Filipino Cops Bound for Iraq by Next Week," *Manila Times*, April 15, 2003, www.manilatimes.net/national/2003/apr/15/top_stories/20030415top2.html (April 8, 2004).

65. Veronica Uy, "RP Humanitarian Team Off to Iraq on May 15," *Inquirer News Service*, April 22, 2003, www.inq7.net/brk/2003/apr/22/text/brkpol_19-1-p.htm (August 29, 2003).

66. Jonathan Hicap, "Bodies of 3 Filipinos Killed in Saudi Bombings Arrive Home," *Manila Times*, June 3, 2003, www.manilatimes.net/national/2003/jun/03/top_stories/20030602top6.html (March 31, 2004).

67. Karl Kaufman, Ma. Theresa Torres, Jowie Corpuz, and Ferdinand Patinio, "US Warns of New Attacks," *Manila Times*, May 16, 2003, www.manilatimes.net/national/2003/may/16/top_stories/20030516top1.html (March 31, 2004).

68. Marichu Villanueva, "RP to Keep Peace Contingent in Iraq," *Philippine Star*, October 20, 2003, www.philstar.com/philstar (November 14, 2003).

69. Villanueva, "RP to Keep Peace."

70. Maricel Cruz and Jowie Corpuz, "Filipino Driver Freed by Iraqi Kidnappers," *Manila Times*, April 14, 2004, www.manilatimes.net/national/2004/apr/14/yehey/top_stories/20040414top4.html (April 13, 2004).

71. David Cagahastian, "Filipino Worker Dies in Iraqi Rebel Ambush," *Manila Bulletin Online*, May 1, 2004, www.mb.com.ph/issues/2004/05/01/MAIN2004050 18542_print.html (July 29, 2004).

72. Jowie Corpus, "No Jobs Yet for Filipino Workers to Rebuild Iraq," *Manila Times*, July 13, 2003, www.manilatimes.net/national/2003/jul/13/top_stories/2003 0713top12.html (March 26, 2004).

73. Philippine Overseas Employment Administration, "OFW Advisory," August 20, 2003, www.poea.gov.ph/html/advisory_nojobsiraq.html (August 20, 2003).

74. Ferdie Maglalang, "Government Suspends Sending of RP Workers to Iraq," *Manila Bulletin Online*, May 5, 2004, www.mb.com.ph/issues/2004/05/05/MAIN 200405058817_print.html (July 29, 2004).

5

THE "PEACE ON TERROR"

Be transformed by the renewing of your minds,
so that you may discern what is the will of God—
what is good and acceptable and perfect.

Romans 12:2

Throughout the postwar occupation of Iraq, President Macapagal-Arroyo publicly remained firm in her decision to support the U.S.-led effort—this, despite a series of escalating suiciding bombings and attacks in Iraq. Within months of the cessation of combat operations, rebels began to target coalition military forces and civilians engaged in reconstruction efforts. The next few months would witness an increased escalation of attacks. Strategically, the abductors were attempting to weaken the Coalition of the Willing.

Throughout 2003 and the first half of 2004, Macapagal-Arroyo worried that a major crisis would develop. As of July, there were an estimated forty-two hundred Filipinos working in Iraq, mostly as cooks, truck drivers, and maintenance technicians. Thousands more workers were based *outside* Iraq but working in the war-torn country, with most driving trucks or working other assorted jobs with construction firms. Employers based in neighboring countries reportedly offered to pay triple salaries to Filipinos willing to deliver shipments into and out of Iraq.

On July 7, a Filipino truck driver, later identified as forty-six-year-old Angelo de la Cruz, was abducted near Fallujah in Iraq. During the attack, his Iraqi security guard was killed. The Arab television channel Al-Jazeera broadcast a videotape showing three armed men standing behind a seated hostage. A banner identified the group as the Iraqi Islamic Army—Khaled bin al-Waleed Corps. This was apparently the first episode involving the group, which took the name Khaled bin al-Waleed from one of the commanders of the army of the Prophet Muhammad. Unless the Philippines removed all of its military and police personnel from Iraq within seventy-two hours, the abductors would behead the hostage. Defense secretary Eduardo Ermita said that the department saw no reason to withdraw the peacekeeping contingent.[1]

The kidnaping of de la Cruz was not the first such crisis confronting the Philippines. As indicated in chapter 4, in April 2004, a Filipino truck driver—along with eight other workers from Pakistan, Turkey, Nepal, India, and Iran—were abducted by Iraqi gunmen. Within a week, however, these hostages were released unharmed. In a written statement, Macapagal-Arroyo expressed relief over the release, adding, "I am directing the [Department of Foreign Affairs] to ensure maximum protective measures for our peacekeeping contingent in Iraq."[2]

At the time of the de la Cruz abduction, the Philippines had, reportedly, a peacekeeping contingent of fifty-one personnel. On learning of the abduction, Senator Villar indicated that his predictions of dire consequences of the Philippines' involvement in Iraq had come true. Interestingly, although he described the presence of Filipino troops in Iraq as the biggest foreign policy error of the present administration, he also said, "Now that a Filipino has been held hostage, we cannot decide to suddenly withdraw our contingent or repatriate our workers from Iraq because that would look like we were giving in to blackmail."[3]

Initially, neither the president nor other top-ranking officials in the Defense Department favored withdrawing the peacekeeping force. However, Macapagal-Arroyo did order an immediate ban on civilian workers traveling to Iraq. Ironically, the announcement arrived just as 120 Filipino workers, hired by a Dubai-based contractor, were set to depart to Iraq. These workers were later permitted to continue to Dubai.

Negotiations were underway by July 10 to secure the release of de la Cruz. Foreign affairs secretary Delia Albert indicated that the Middle East Preparedness Team was handling the situation after the Philippine charge d'affaires to Iraq, Eric Endaya, established contact with the Iraqi insurgents. Roy Cimatu, special envoy and chief of the Philippines' Middle East Preparedness Team was sent to negotiate. In a statement, Macapagal-Arroyo said that the country was at its "most crucial and sensitive point." While asking the media to tone down reports, presidential spokespersons also gave no indication that there was a possibility of withdrawing the Filipino troops.[4]

By Sunday, as the deadline was approaching, Philippine officials attempted to persuade the abductors that if they freed de la Cruz, the Philippines would pull out their troops by August 20, the scheduled date of their return. Albert reaffirmed that the government's policy was to retain the humanitarian mission in Iraq until its scheduled return. Presidential spokesperson Ignacio Bunye likewise said, "Our future actions shall be guided by the UN Security Council decision as embodied in Resolution 1546, which defines the role of the UN and its member states in the future of Iraq." National security advisor Norberto Gonzales indicated also that the administration was in consultation with influential Muslim leaders in several countries to talk with de la Cruz's captors and explain the Philippines' position. Gonzales also said that the government would exhaust all channels to free de la Cruz without sacrificing the Philippine commitment to the U.S.-led coalition.[5]

Efforts were underway outside of the Philippines. United Nations Secretary-General Kofi Annan called on the Iraqi militants to release de la Cruz. In a statement released by the Department of Foreign Affairs, Annan called for the release of de la Cruz as well as two Bulgarians who had been reportedly kidnapped. The UN secretary-general asked for an end to the threat to innocent civilians who were being abducted for political ends.[6] Concomitant, Gonzales said that the administration had asked influential Muslim leaders in several countries to intervene on their behalf. According to Gonzales, "We have talked with the highest religious [leaders] in Indonesia, Malaysia, Libya and Egypt."[7]

Problems were compounded on Sunday when the New People's Army (NPA)—the military branch of the Communist Party of the Philippines (CPP)—announced that it would lead moves to overthrow the Macapagal-Arroyo administration if de la Cruz was beheaded. In a statement, CPP spokesperson Gregorio Rosal accused the president of sacrificing the lives of overseas Filipino workers by supporting the U.S.-backed invasion of Iraq. He stated, "The Arroyo regime is responsible for putting the lives of Filipino workers in Iraq and the Middle East in danger. . . . It is the full responsibility of the puppet Arroyo government whatever happens to de la Cruz. The moment his head is severed, we will do everything to ensure that the Arroyo government will be overthrown."[8] Likewise, the Moro-Christian People's Alliance demanded that Macapagal-Arroyo withdraw the troops to save de la Cruz's life. Datu Cosain Naga, the alliance's leader, said, "With the U.S. being isolated in the international community for waging a unilateral and unjustified war in Iraq, the Philippines is committed to no community but to the U.S. government alone." His comments were in response to earlier remarks by members of the administration who were concerned over the "repercussions" of withdrawing from the coalition.[9]

U.S. officials expressed their concern and support. U.S. Ambassador to the Philippines Francis Ricciardone praised the Macapagal-Arroyo administration throughout the early days of the crisis. In reference to the president, Ricciardone said, "I see a leader who has strength and compassion in a way that is truly inspirational here. It's a tough crisis, and leaders are called upon in a crisis to do hard things." He added, "She has shown deep, deep care for this hostage, and also cared for the country's long-term interest."

On Monday, it was reported that a nine-day reprieve had been secured for de la Cruz. A senior diplomat in Baghdad said, "The deadline has been extended . . . till July 20. This has given us hope that the hostage is alive and the kidnappers are realizing that he [de la Cruz] has nothing [against them]." In actuality, this was a second reprieve; on Saturday night, the abductors had extended the deadline by twenty-four hours, according to a statement broadcast on Al-Jazeera television. The abductors did, however, reaffirm their threat of killing de la Cruz unless the Philippines withdrew its peacekeeping contingent. Sunday night, the Cabinet Oversight Committee on Internal Security met for three hours and decided to stand by its commitment to keep the mission in Iraq until August 20. Officials of the Macapagal-Arroyo administration, however, declined to comment further, instead maintaining a blackout on most information.[10]

Other events transpired over the weekend that added to the surrealism of the crisis. On Saturday morning, labor secretary Patricia Sto. Tomas announced that de la Cruz had been released. She had told the media that de la Cruz was being taken to a Baghdad hotel to be turned over to Philippine officials. Within hours, however, the Iraqi insurgents who were holding de la Cruz hostage denied reports of his release. In an interview, Sto. Tomas admitted her mistake and apologized for her premature announcement. Consequently, neither Macapagal-Arroyo nor Bunye would issue any statement. Bunye, instead, maintained that only the Department of Foreign Affairs was authorized to provide information on the situation. The department, however, also declined to give any information about the negotiations underway. When questioned on the blackout, Albert simply said, "We ask for the understanding of the nation and the media for us to proceed with the task at hand away from the media spotlight. We shall endeavor, as best as we can and as circumstances permit, to keep the people informed of crucial developments."[11]

Not all sectors of the Philippine government were silent. Roberto Romulo, chair of the Task Force on the Reconstruction of Iraq, said that pullout or no pullout, the Philippines would continue to get an equal chance in the bidding of contracts. Romulo explained that the Philippines' future business interest in Iraq was not among the worries of the government in deciding if it would send home the fifty-one Filipino troops. He said, "I don't believe there would be any punishment."[12]

Tuesday brought news that further complicated the situation. It was announced, first, that the government offered to pay a ransom to the Iraqi militants in exchange for de la Cruz's release. Details were withheld as to how much ransom was offered and even if it was to come from the Philippine government or some other source. The abductors, however, apparently rejected the offer, indicating that they would hold to their demands. According to an unspecified diplomat, "The captors are committed to their cause and said they cannot be bought."[13] Concurrently, a top official of the National Democratic Front of the Philippines, the political party of the CPP that is based in the Netherlands, warned the Macapagal-Arroyo administration that the outcome of the de la Cruz incident could jeopardize the government's peace negotiations with the communists. These statements were apparently unconnected with the earlier threats of the NPA. According to Luis Jalandoni, chair of the front, the Macapagal-Arroyo administration had to act immediately to comply with its obligation to defend and protect the lives and the rights of Filipino migrant workers. Jalandoni condemned the Macapagal-Arroyo administration for its "subservience to US imperialism."[14] Peace talks between the Philippine government and the National Democratic Front of the Philippines were set for August. Talks had stalled, however, for numerous reasons, not the least of which was the designation of the CPP–NPA, as well as Jose Sison, as "terrorists." Such a listing would severely hamper any efforts to broker a peace settlement.

The surrealism surrounding the abduction of de la Cruz continued as it was announced on Wednesday that eight Filipino peacekeepers had already been withdrawn from the initial contingent of fifty-one.[15] Unidentified diplomats in the Philippines expressed their frustration over the Macapagal-Arroyo administration's secrecy. According to one official, "By delivering vague, ambiguous statements the government is playing a dangerous game. No one knows where it stands." Shuhei Ogawa, press officer of the Japanese Embassy in Manila said, "We are waiting for further explanation from the Philippine government if such statements [the removal of eight peacekeepers] actually mean a pullout ahead of the planned schedule on August 20. We are aware of those statements . . . but we have not received any explanation on the meaning of the statement."[16]

By Thursday, July 15, it was announced that the Philippine government had indeed negotiated for the release of de la Cruz. Albert, in a statement read on local television, explained, "The Philippine government has recalled the head of the Philippine humanitarian contingent in Iraq. He is leaving Iraq today with 10 members of the Philippine humanitarian contingent." She continued, "The rest of the members of the contingent will be out of Iraq shortly. Efforts continue to secure the safe release of Angelo." The statement caught many officials off-guard. U.S. Ambassador to the Philippines Francis Ricciardone indicated that Macapagal-Arroyo had assured him that there would be no pullout of Philippines forces. Ricciardone said of the decision, "We were not happy with the direction of the change overnight. We were quite surprise by that statement when it came out."[17]

Within days of arranging for de la Cruz's release, Macapagal-Arroyo said that divine "intercession" was at hand. She explained, "I have sought Our Lady's intercession many times, and once again she interceded. This time, she interceded for a defining decision in my presidency and in my life as a Filipino."[18]

GLOBAL REACTIONS

In the aftermath of Macapagal-Arroyo's decision, the governments of Singapore, Poland, Australia, and the United States were quick to condemn the Philippine government. The consensus was that any attempt to negotiate with terrorists would embolden them and contribute to increased attacks. Ruth Urry, assistant information officer of the U.S. Embassy in Manila, issued a one-page statement indicating that the United States was dismayed by the actions of the Philippine government. She said, "This decision sends the wrong signal."[19] Afterward, Ricciardone, the U.S. ambassador to the Philippines, added, "In a time of crisis an ally, a friend, helps a partner to be strong and that's what we are trying to do. In the time of crisis it's up to us as your allies to help you be strong, to encourage you." However, the ambassador also urged the Philippine government not to "confuse your enemies with your friends." Apparently, Ricciardone had been in consultation with the president regarding her decision. In Washington, State Department spokesperson Richard Boucher said that the decision of the Philippines was unexpected, adding, "We think that withdrawal sends the wrong signal and that it is important for the people to stand up to terrorists and not allow them to change our behavior."[20]

U.S. Secretary of State Colin Powell likewise rebuked the Philippine government for its decision to withdraw its forces. Speaking before the U.S. Institute of Peace, Powell said, "This kind of action cannot be allowed to succeed anywhere in the 21st century, above all not Iraq." In turn, Powell praised South Korea and Bulgaria for "not blinking and not faltering even though they are being tested mightily by kidnappings and by beheadings."[21]

Donald Rumsfeld, U.S. defense secretary, was equally blunt, telling reporters at a Pentagon press conference that "weakness is provocative." He continued, "Sovereign nations make sovereign decisions just as people do. If you want more of something you reward it and if you want less of it you penalize it."

The Australian reaction was more adamant. Australia's foreign minister, Alexander Downer, called on the Philippine ambassador to Canberra, Cristina Ortega, to convey his "extreme disappointment." Downer branded the Macapagal-Arroyo administration's decision as "marshmallowlike."[22] Chris Kenny, spokesperson for Downer, added that the Australian government attempted to persuade the Macapagal-Arroyo administration to remain firm to its commitment. Kenny elaborates, "If countries give in to terrorists, it will only encourage them to kidnap more hostages in an attempt to change the foreign policies of countries. Australia could not and would never do that."[23]

The Singaporean government, in expressing its disappointment in the Philippines' actions, remained firm in its resolve to maintain its thirty-three-personnel force in Iraq. Tony Tan, Singapore coordinating minister for security and defense, said, "The Singapore government cannot and should never negotiate with terrorists. That would encourage more terrorists to take more of our people as hostages."[24]

The reactions of foreign governments to the decision of Macapagal-Arroyo were almost without exception grounded in political realism. This is especially true of "Western" governments or those with strong ties to the West (e.g., Singapore). Statements generally viewed the crisis as a test, downplaying if not ignoring the life-or-death implications. Australian prime minister John Howard, for example, described the situation in Hobbesian terms, saying that, while he could understand the anguish of people in the Philippine government dealing with families of the hostage, "It's a wretched state of affairs but if you give in you won't stop it happening again."[25]

And it did happen again. On July 23, seven hostages—three Kenyans, three Indians, and an Egyptian—were abducted.[26] The abductors threatened to behead the men if their countries did not withdraw their troops and citizens from Iraq. Ironically, none of the hostages' governments had been part of the Coalition of the Willing. They were, however, truck drivers working for a Kuwaiti company. The abductors warned that every Kuwaiti company dealing with Americans would "be dealt with as an American."[27]

A second kidnaping was reported by July 25; this time, a senior Egyptian diplomat was taken hostage. The abductors demanded that Egypt give up any plans to send security experts to support Iraq's government. Egypt, which declined to send military forces, had offered to train Iraqi police and security personnel in Egypt.[28] And on July 26, a group vowed to bomb Australia unless it withdrew its forces from Iraq. Downer said that the increased terrorist threats were the direct result of the Philippines' decision (as well as Spain's pullout earlier in the year).[29]

At this point, it remains clear that the decision of Macapagal-Arroyo potentially damaged the international relations of the Philippines. Officials within the Philippines and without have speculated that the potential losses associated with the decision would far outweigh any potential gains. Was the decision, therefore, related primarily to domestic concerns?

DOMESTIC/FOREIGN POLICIES

In the days following Macapagal-Arroyo's decision, analysts believed that the president's decision was an attempt to strengthen her domestic front even if it weakened her international standing.[30] Clearly, Macapagal-Arroyo was confronted with a dizzying array of domestic problems, many of which were intimately associated with foreign affairs. I consider two in particular.

Insurgencies and Separatist Movements

As de la Cruz was being released, another hostage situation was unfolding in the Philippines. This one concerned two soldiers of the Armed Forces of the Philippines (AFP) who were being held by members of the NPA. Spokespersons for the NPA requested the AFP to suspend military operations in three provinces in the Bicol region in exchange for the release of the soldiers. This request was an attempt by the NPA to take advantage of the government's apparent changed stance against terrorism.[31] Lieutenant Colonel Daniel Lucero of the AFP, however, explained, "We don't negotiate with terrorists." He explained that suspending military operations against insurgents and national security threats was against the AFP's policy. "We would like to tell these NPA rebels that terrorism doesn't work in the country."[32]

This hostage crisis came in the wake of another act of violence. One week earlier, an AFP sergeant was killed in an ambush by a suspected NPA hit man in Nueva Ecija. The shooting came just days after NPA spokesperson Rosal had warned the government of more NPA offensives if the administration failed to secure the safety of de la Cruz.[33]

Macapagal-Arroyo was also attempting to deal with the Islamic separatist movements in the southern Philippines, a policy area that had strong connections with the U.S.-led War on Terror. Throughout her administration, Macapagal-Arroyo had attempted to broker a peace settlement with the Moro Islamic Liberation Front (see chapter 1). The government of Malaysia had been serving as an intermediary government in the ongoing negotiations. Settlement talks, however, were routinely delayed. Indeed, the lack of progress in reaching a settlement carried material implications with the United States. The United States had allocated $30 million for development projects in the southern Philippines, pending a peace agreement. However, the apparent intransigence of the talks led the United States to rescind the entire offer. On July 8, before the de la Cruz incident, Ricciardone voiced Washington's concern about the need to strengthen the rule of law in the Philippines to improve the chances of solving the problems of insurgency and poverty. According to Ricciardone, "There was no serious peace process. It's always 'next month there'll be a meeting.' . . . The money has been shifted to places and other programs of Mindanao such as small-scale infrastructure." In response, Bunye said, "We acknowledge the concern of the U.S. government, but we do not have to be told to do our duty."[34]

Senator Aquilino Pimentel reacted strongly to the decision of the United States to reallocate the funds. He urged the Macapagal-Arroyo administration to replace Malaysia as the third-party intermediary and instead turn toward the United States. He said, "It's about time the government refocuses its energies toward having the Americans broker the peace talks. We have given enough time for Malaysia to do its part, but unfortunately nothing is happening." He indicated, furthermore, that the Bush administration had sent exploratory missions to the Philippines and Malaysia to see how Washington could more actively participate in the peace negotiations.[35]

After the decision of Macapagal-Arroyo to remove the peacekeeping forces, Pimentel urged the president to mend the strained ties between the Philippines and the United States. In a statement, Pimentel explained, "It would be sheer hypocrisy if the administration would pretend that it's business as usual in our dealings with the United States and we have nothing to worry about." Indeed, he indicated that an overall reassessment of Philippines–U.S. relations was in order in the wake of apprehensions that

Washington would scale down or eliminate development and other aid as punishment.[36]

It did not help matters, furthermore, when a Brussels-based think tank called International Crisis Group described the Philippines as crucial to the evolving terrorist threat in Southeast Asia. As indicated in earlier chapters, the United States has consistently viewed Southeast Asia as the "Second Front" in the "War on Terror." Accordingly, the Philippines is poised to become the key piece in a renewed domino theory of international (terror) relations. The group's report—released on July 14, as the de la Cruz incident was unfolding—emphasized the connections between the Moro Islamic Liberation Front and the al Qaeda–lined Jemaah Islamiah group.[37] Macapagal-Arroyo was in a difficult position to broker a peace settlement while not appearing "soft" on terrorism.

This was not the first time that U.S. officials had interfered in the Philippines' "domestic" war against insurgencies. Nor was this the first time that U.S. officials had questioned the Philippines' resolve in its War on Terror. According to James Kelly, U.S. assistant of state for Asia and Pacific affairs, the threat of terrorism was "greatest" in Southeast Asia, "particularly in the Philippines and Indonesia." His comments came in October 2003 and were made in a speech before the Industrial College of the Armed Forces of the Philippines. Kelly said that Washington was "interested in a sustainable peace that will address the legitimate grievances of the Muslim population, a peace that will calm the situation in Mindanao and make the area less attractive to radical influence."[38] In November 2003, the U.S. Defense Department identified the Philippines as a "high-risk" country, one where there was a big possibility of a terrorist attack. In response, Macapagal-Arroyo said, "The probability of terrorist attacks is spread all over and does not help putting countries like the Philippines in a list of potential targets as if others are free from this threat." She continued, "Quiet international cooperation will work much better than this labeling exercise."[39] And in February, a U.S.-based travel risk management firm likewise listed the Philippines as one of the top countries vulnerable to terrorism. Philippine Department of Foreign Affairs spokesperson Jula Heidemann said, "I think it is unfair. That is their opinion. It is a private thing that has no basis at all."[40]

Perhaps Macapagal-Arroyo and other officials were concerned not so much as being identified as a terrorist threat but as being seen "soft" on terrorism. Statements by U.S. officials in the months ahead would give any government reason to pause. Nowhere is this better expressed than in Bush's 2004 State of the Union address. Speaking after the campaigns in

Afghanistan and Iraq, Bush noted that "the leader of Libya voluntarily pledged to disclose and dismantle all of his regime's weapons of mass destruction programs." Bush continued, "Nine months of intense negotiations involving the United States and Great Britain succeed with Libya, while 12 years of diplomacy with Iraq did not. And one reason is clear: *For diplomacy to be effective, words must be credible, and no one can now doubt the word of America*" (italics added).[41] The message is clear: Stand with the United States or suffer the consequences. No doubt Macapagal-Arroyo has not forgotten an apparent "diplomatic reproach" from the United States. In April 2004, the *New York Times* ran an article about the Bush administration's silent reprimand of Macapagal-Arroyo for her "soft" campaign against terrorism. Ironically, the article mentioned that the Philippines had failed to act on several intelligence reports about terrorist activities provided by the United States. Macapagal-Arroyo, at the time, dismissed the reports as purely "fictitious."[42]

The implied use of U.S. military force—regardless of international recognition, legitimacy, or evidence—was fundamental to the Coalition of the Willing, and it remains a viable threat to maintain control over foreign governments. Moreover, Macapagal-Arroyo's relationship with the AFP in the campaigns against insurgencies and separatism could very easily combine with U.S. geopolitical interests in the region. Was the decision of Macapagal-Arroyo to withdraw troops, therefore, related to the threats of the CPP–NPA? If so, then her attempts to broker a peace with these movements would intensify another, perhaps more serious issue to her presidency: the threat of a military coup.

Threats of the Armed Forces of the Philippines

On July 27, 2003, approximately three hundred junior officers of the AFP staged a coup in an attempt to depose Macapagal-Arroyo. In staging the mutiny, the Magdaló group seized the Oakwood Premiere service apartments in Makati City. The mutineers surrendered within twenty-four hours. In the subsequent months, the mutineers maintained that the attempted coup was a spontaneous act prompted by corruption in government and poor management of the military. The mutiny came one day after Macapagal-Arroyo had ordered the AFP leadership to capture Lieutenant Sergeant Antonio Trillianes and five other junior officers for allegedly deserting their posts and carting away high-powered firearms. In October, however, a six-person civilian fact-finding commission known as the Feliciano Commission concluded that the Oakwood mutiny was part of a larger conspiracy to seize power from the government by restoring ousted President Joseph Estrada and then appointing a fifteen-member government council. This was according to a plan authored by opposition Senator Gregorio Honasan. This was not Honasan's first attempt at a power grab. Before becoming a senator, Honasan had led a coup against former president Corazon Aquino.[43]

Given the continued opposition to Macapagal-Arroyo from Estrada supporters, a disgruntled military—or even a small component of the military—does not bode well. Moreover, to the extent that the AFP of the Philippines does not share the same philosophy of the president in terms of the War on Terror compounds the problem. In particular, Macapagal-Arroyo, following the de la Cruz incident, looks even more "soft" on terror—a charge, as we have seen, that has already been labeled on her administration. A military coup—perhaps with the support of U.S. forces under the guise of combating terrorism—remains an all-too real possibility.

I have argued to this point that, from a political realist position, the decision of Macapagal-Arroyo does not make sense. Certainly, her support of de la Cruz and her overall attempt to be a "friend" of the Filipino people remain as factors. This argument, though, must be tempered by the fact that Macapagal-Arroyo is not eligible to run for a second term as president because of term limits. Therefore, her main concern would not be future presidential elections, the next being in 2010. Macapagal-Arroyo may be most concerned about increased attacks by the CPP–NPA and, perhaps, by Islamic separatist groups such as the Abu Sayyaf Group. Her decision to acquiesce to the demands of the Iraqi insurgents would potentially alleviate this risk. Unfortunately, this would further alienate the president from the AFP. In recent months, it has been the AFP that has aggressively pursued a military campaign against both the CPP–NPA and the Moro Islamic Liberation Front. Differences between the AFP and the president lead to the unappealing threat of a military coup.

How, then, are we to understand the decision making of Macapagal-Arroyo? If we follow the statements of Ricciardone, the Philippine president made the decision to spare the life of de la Cruz overnight, after having assured the U.S. ambassador that she would not give in to the demands of the Iraqi militants. I suggest that Macapagal-Arroyo's decision was not based on any argument that conforms with realist politics. Instead, Macapagal-Arroyo's actions were determined by her political fundamentalism and thus were ultimately decided by a Catholic sense of justice and not domestic or foreign policy considerations.

THE MORALITY OF OCCUPATION

A week after the release of de la Cruz, Macapagal-Arroyo addressed the Department of Foreign Affairs. The president reaffirmed her "eight realities" of foreign policy but, as expected, stressed two in particular: the reality of the United States and the reality of overseas Filipinos. She explained that she committed the Philippines to join the fight against global terrorism that erupted as a result of the September 11 tragedy in the United States. As to the war in Iraq, Macapagal-Arroyo was more circumspect. She did not, for example, speak of the regime change of Saddam Hussein, neither did she speak of weapons of mass destruction. Instead, Macapagal-Arroyo indicated simply that the Philippines had committed a small humanitarian and peacekeeping force of one hundred persons to help in its post-war reconstruction. She explained further that the Philippines was in a special circumstance. "Unlike the U.S., Australia, Bulgaria and other countries," she said, "we have 1.5 million Filipinos who live and work in the Middle East and 4,000 are working in Iraq." From the Philippine president's perspective, she had a responsibility to consider the welfare of these workers, and she hoped that foreign governments would understand these circumstances. However, Macapagal-Arroyo was not going to defend her decision to remove the peacekeeping forces. She declared bluntly, "What I have said to you today, it won't take more than three lines to summarize, and let me say these three lines: One, I take sole responsibility. Two, I make no apologies. Three, I stuck to my oath."[44]

Toward the end of her speech, Macapagal-Arroyo made the following statement: "Because there are many ways to show our commitment, our Filipino people and our nation remain committed to our friends and allies abroad while remaining true to our convictions here at home. *We share the same goal but do not always walk on the same path*" (italics added).[45] This phrase is crucial in that it directs attention to a divergence of opinion between Macapagal-Arroyo and the U.S.-led coalition. It is therefore instructive, first, to consider the motivation behind Macapagal-Arroyo's decision to join the Coalition of the Willing and, subsequently, to isolate four specific points of divergence between the Philippines' position and that of the broader coalition.

STEPS ALONG A DIFFERENT PATH

At the Basilica of the National Shrine of the Immaculate Conception in Washington, D.C., Macapagal-Arroyo delivered a speech during a mass for the victims of the September 11 tragedy. She began by extending her condolences to those who suffered and her praise to the "indomitable spirit and the courage and faith that have always been the hallmark of America." She then said, "In these trying times, we must unite in our efforts to renew the human spirit and out of faith in God to rise above our grief." Her speech was not a quest for vengeance. Unlike Bush's invocation of Psalm 23, Macapagal-Arroyo counseled a path of solidarity. She explained that the Philippines had been fighting terrorism: "What we were fighting in isolation in the southwestern part of the Philippines is now a common fight. It is regrettable that it takes a tragedy to bring the community of nations together, but it has." In effect, Macapagal-Arroyo is indicating that numerous efforts to combat terrorism were underway *prior* to the United States' post–September 11 stance. With reference to Malaysia and Indonesia, Macapagal-Arroyo explained, "This is a war that must be bereft of any religious undertones, and therefore the Philippines has institutionalized the tools of autonomy, consensus and interfaith dialogue with our Muslim brothers. The terrorists want to make this a religious war. We must make this an opportunity to have religious understanding."[46] The position of Macapagal-Arroyo is consistent with recent moves by the Catholic church to bring about interfaith dialogue.

The message of Macapagal-Arroyo was consistent with a Catholic vision of peace. The path laid out by the Philippine president was premised on the *salvation* of lives through the promotion of peace. This position of Macapagal-Arroyo was clearly expressed weeks before the attacks of September 11. Speaking at the Twenty-first National Prayer Breakfast, Macapagal-Arroyo specified her work ethic as being guided by the philosophy of doing what is right. However, she explained, "To do what is right, I need prayer to discern what is right." She continued, "God's taking care of the rest when we do what is right and do our best can . . . be summed up in the article of faith that all things work for the good of those who have a covenant with the Lord."[47]

Macapagal-Arroyo continued: "While I do not believe in fate, I believe in divine providence. And as leaders of society, we are placed where we are because of a reason, because of a plan, a divine plan for all of us. And each one of us must pray to discern what that plan is, then act according to our best light to comply with that plan." The president then explained, "The key in manifesting God's plan in our lives lies in our ability through prayer to discern his divine wisdom and to apply it in our daily lives." It was this application that Macapagal-Arroyo attempted to integrate into her administration. And it was in this context that Macapagal-Arroyo understood the path of her administration. Macapagal-Arroyo referred to 2 Chronicles 7:14, when the Lord said, "If my people, who are called by my name, will humble themselves and pray and seek my face and turn from their wicked ways, then I will hear from heaven and will forgive their sin and will heal their land." Macapagal-Arroyo explained that, for her, "'to humble ourselves' [means] staying detached from the trappings and perks of power. It means reaching out to those who still carry hatred or cynicism in their hearth. It means forgiving those who have done wrong rather than using my power to do vengeance upon them."[48] The path adopted by Macapagal-Arroyo to "fight" the War against Terror was thus founded on certain moral teachings, namely, those of peace, reconciliation, and solidarity. Actual war, while a possibility, was to be avoided if possible through alternative means. Indeed, in direct reference to the Catholic model of just war, Macapagal-Arroyo explained in August 2003 that "peace cannot be limited to a mere absence of war" and that "the will of the people and God is always ascendant in the search for peace."[49]

PEACE, RECONCILIATION, AND SOLIDARITY

Macapagal-Arroyo's Foundation Day speech on July 23, 2004, provides important insights into the intentions undergirding the Philippine president's decision. In reference to U.S.–Philippine international relations, Macapagal-Arroyo explained, "The last three years in particular saw a close partnership between the Philippines and the United States. I'm pleased that the Philippines and the U.S. embarked on broad security cooperation to address the issues of terrorism, illegal narcotics trade, human trafficking and other transnational crimes."[50] Significantly, Macapagal-Arroyo did not mention at this point the war in Iraq. This suggests that Macapagal-Arroyo was not a strong supporter of the *war* against Iraq, although she did support the underlying premise of humanitarian intervention. As detailed in chapter 4, Macapagal-Arroyo believed that sufficient cause existed to effect regime change in Iraq. Personally, she may have held out hope that Saddam could be removed peaceably, as Marcos had been in 1986 and Estrada in 2001; the latter change, of course, saw Macapagal-Arroyo ascend to the presidency.

It is perhaps not surprising that Macapagal-Arroyo would focus on solidarity and reconciliation in light of her political career. However, these have been consistent themes, suggesting that her pronouncements are more than political expediency. A statement released by the president during the Holy Week of 2004 expressed simply,

> There is no more I can ask for on this day than for peace and solidarity among our people. Let us celebrate the Holy Week in the tone of sacrifice, forgiveness and concern for one another. Let us make it a time to contemplate the blessings that have come our way from the Almighty: the wholeness of our families, the peace of our communities and the unity of the Filipino despite the trials of a harsh and uncertain world.[51]

This prayer was delivered during the months of intensified insurgent operations in Iraq as well as continued insurgencies and military campaigns in the Philippines. Her focus was that of sacrifice and forgiveness, both of which were crucial to foster peace and solidarity. It was a continuation of her quest for reconciliation. In November 2003, for example, Macapagal-Arroyo delivered a speech during the Twenty-second Philippines National Prayer Breakfast. She began by noting that there is no substitute for living and leading in God's presence and for calling on His holy name for help or thanksgiving. For the country to move forward, though, she stressed the need for reconciliation. She then asked rhetorically, "What is principled reconciliation?" She informed her audience that the previous day she called her cabinet to a special meting to reflect on this question. In attendance at the cabinet meeting was Reverend Archbishop Capalla, incoming president of the Catholic Bishops Conference of the Philippines. Out of the meeting Macapagal-Arroyo came away with her understanding of principled reconciliation, namely, "the call of God to our people today." She explained, "The people must sense a unifying force in their institutions of governance or they themselves will be divided and weakened in facing the formidable challenges of waging the peace and fighting poverty." Quoting 2 Peter 1:5, Macapagal-Arroyo said, "We are told to put forth 'Earnest effort in supplying virtue to our faith.' Earnest effort to me . . . [means] we need to speed up the healing process."[52] At this point, it is obvious that these scriptures exert a tremendous influence on the day-to-day workings of the Macapagal-Arroyo administration. Her statements reflect the depth to which she turns to the Lord for answers.

The Old Testament includes numerous stories of prophets who discerned the will of God. And it turn, God chose people to be agents of discernment.[53] Macapagal-Arroyo continued in her speech with a story of being called away to give a prayer. At the time, she was in a crucial command conference and so did not have time to adequately prepare a prayer. She said, "And so, I had to ask the Lord, Lord, what do you want me to pray? And the Lord, in a little voice made me pray: here I am Lord. I have heard you calling me by name. I will go Lord where you lead me. I will hold your people in my heart." This is the approach of Macapagal-Arroyo to her presidency. Speaking to her audience, she said, "I seek your prayers, brothers and sisters, so that we can institute true reforms in our way of politics, in our way of economics to really develop our economy and create a stronger republic to bring about the common good." The common good, as discerned by Macapagal-Arroyo, is "healing and reconciliation." She invoked Psalm 127:1, which reads, "Unless the Lord builds the house, its builders labor in vain." Macapagal-Arroyo explained, "We can only build the strong republic that we want to be the home of our people with the help, in fact, with the lordship of the Lord."[54] This same understanding, I maintain, informed her decision in the reconstruction efforts of Iraq. It was only through the reconciliation efforts through the labors of the Filipino workers that a strong republic could be built. By the time of the de la Cruz incident, the morality underscoring the reconstruction efforts had vanished.

THE VENGEANCE OF BUSH

A fundamental difference between the political fundamentalism of Macapagal-Arroyo and that of Bush lies in the belief of vengeance. This, I contend, is a crucial factor that differentiates the Macapagal-Arroyo administration from that of the United States. Whereas Bush assumes God's will in waging war against Iraq and other countries through a unilateral doctrine of preemptive strike, Macapagal-Arroyo forwards a Catholic understanding of peace defined by development, solidarity, world order, and human rights. The Catholic tradition holds the meaning of peace in positive terms. It must be constructed on the basis of central human values: truth, justice, freedom, and love. Peace is not the absence of war; instead, peace results from harmony built into human society by God and put into practice by people.

The reconstruction efforts of the Philippines were seen to conform with these objectives. Both the deployment of peacekeeping forces and migrant workers also made sense in terms of a neoliberal economic philosophy. Through the deployment of workers, Filipinos could be helped through the provision of jobs, but so also could Iraqis, as migrant workers repaired damaged facilities. The sending of Filipinos to Iraq was not, as Macapagal-Arroyo made clear on many occasions, an opportunity to seek vengeance. It is written in Deuteronomy 32:35, "To Me belongs vengeance, and recompence." Likewise, Romans 12:17–18 asserts, "Recompense to no man evil for evil. Provide things honest in the sight of all men. If it be possible, as much as lies in you, live peaceably with all men." I suggest at this point that Macapagal-Arroyo concluded that the war and occupation of Iraq were conducted under false premises.

Perhaps also she disapproved of the Bush administration's conduct of the War on Terror. Certainly, as discussed in chapter 4, her methods of counterterrorism are largely dissonant with those of the Bush administration. This would lead naturally to differences of opinion when the subject of negotiations arise. In Luke 15:2, Jesus "receives sinners and eats with them." This has important ramifications not only for Macapagal-Arroyo's approach to dealing with the abductors of de la Cruz but also for the ongoing separatist movements in the southern Philippines. Following Catholic teachings, Macapagal-Arroyo forwards a morally informed position of reconciliation and solidarity.

THE SANCTITY OF LIFE

Bush has professed an ethic of respect for innocent human life. However, as Peter Singer finds, the actions of Bush seem to discount this moral position. In particular, during combat operations in both Afghanistan and Iraq, Bush could have ordered the American armed forces to take greater care to avoid civilian deaths—collateral damage.[55] Indeed, Bush might have attempted to work through the United Nations to bring about a nonmilitary solution, one that would have prevented the loss of life associated with war. Instead, Bush pursued war.

A primary motivation for the Bush administration's pursuit of war was revenge: a spectacular display of "shock and awe" capability. Larry Everest writes of September 11, 2001, that the Bush administration was required to *react*. Throughout the twentieth century, American hegemony and global leadership has been defined by its military superiority and its willingness to assert such strength. Everest suggests, therefore, that American credibility was at stake. A rapidly deployed and vastly superior military action was required: Afghanistan fit the bill. However, although related, the Bush administration was able to capitalize on the post–September 11 environment.[56] In particular, advocates of an even more militarist approach by the U.S. government to Middle East politics were able to take advantage of the antiterrorist mobilization to press their case for regime change in Iraq, Saudi Arabia, and Iran.[57]

Macapagal-Arroyo has consistently upheld a moral position in support of the sanctity of life. She explained in her 2004 State of the Nation address,

"I was reflecting whether one life should be sacrificed for no pressing reason or saved by accelerating an on-going pullout."[58] This statement is important because it reiterates the claims made by her administration throughout the crisis, namely, that the Philippines' peacekeeping contingent was already scheduled to leave Iraq within a month. One may also interpret her statement as questioning the overall purpose of peacekeeping forces in Iraq. Thus, she could see "no pressing reason" for the continued presence of Filipino troops. In the final analysis, however, Macapagal-Arroyo's decision conforms with the approach forwarded by Pope John Paul II, namely, that the rights of one individual are to take precedence over those of the collective nation. Macapagal-Arroyo at this point embodied an ethic that values the dignity of the person over sovereign states or collective consequences.[59]

Arguably, one of the more significant statements announced by Macapagal-Arroyo was her claim "I did not sacrifice policy to save a human life." She said that she "applied policy for that purpose" and that "the Philippines has no policy that demands sacrifice of human lives." Her statement is even more significant when one considers the decades of criticism leveled against successive administrations for "sacrificing" overseas Filipino workers for capital accumulation (see chapter 2).

Macapagal-Arroyo's decision to "save" de la Cruz was given additional moral authority through various church spokespersons. Bishop Efraim Tendero, secretary-general of the Philippine Council of Evangelical Churches likened the decision of Macapagal-Arroyo to Jesus's "Parable of the Lost Sheep."[60] In Luke 15:4–7 Jesus explains, "Suppose one of you has a hundred sheep and loses one of them. Does he not leave the ninety-nine in the wilderness and go after the lost sheep until he finds it? And when he finds it, he joyfully puts it on his shoulders and goes home. Then he calls his friends and neighbors together and says, 'Rejoice with me; I have found my lost sheep.' I tell you that in the same way there will be more rejoicing in heaven over one sinner who repents than over ninety-nine righteous persons who do not need to repent." Indeed, Macapagal-Arroyo declared in a statement released on July 20, "Every life is important. Angelo was spared, and we rejoice."[61]

In this analogy, de la Cruz was not a sinner, but he was lost and did require the shepherd, Macapagal-Arroyo, to go after him. As to the other ninety-nine sheep, I suggest that these represent the other workers deployed to Iraq. For Macapagal-Arroyo, the immediacy of the situation was clear: Through negotiation—which we have established is Macapagal-Arroyo's preferential strategy—her decision could prevent the death of de la Cruz.

The risk is that later, other workers may be placed in jeopardy. But at the time, the other ninety-nine sheep, so to speak, were not in trouble; they did not require saving. Bishop Tendero, in conclusion, praised Macapagal-Arroyo's "Christian act of valuing one human life" over "the interests of commerce" and "the agenda of diplomats."[62] This, again, conforms with the Vatican's stance on human rights.

INNOCENCE LOST

It is understood that soldiers will die in wars. Politicians and generals may attempt to develop technologies and minimize casualties, but, as Napoleon once said, "soldiers are made to be killed." Not so for noncombatants. Within a just war, states remain committed to defend these rights whether wars are aggressive or not.[63]

As the war against Iraq was rapidly unfolding, Rumsfeld called Bush and said that they had information that Saddam Hussein and his sons would be in a particular location; Rumsfeld wanted permission to bomb the site. Bush later explained in an interview with Tom Brokaw,

> I was hesitant at first, to be frank with you, because I was worried that the first pictures coming out of Iraq would be a wounded grandchild of Saddam Hussein . . . that the first images of the American attack would be death to young children.[64]

Peter Singer suggests that the concern Bush expresses here is not about the risk that American bombs might kill or wound children—who would, even if they were Hussein's grandchildren, be innocent of his crimes. It was that Bush was concerned about potential negative reactions to the war. In other words, Bush was willing to risk the killing and maiming of innocent Iraqis in an attempt to *perhaps* kill Saddam Hussein. We might also note that such a preemptive strike says volume about the motivations: the goal was not simply "regime change" and the bringing of Saddam Hussein to justice before an international court of law. Instead, the purpose was the killing of Hussein.

Macapagal-Arroyo, like Bush, was confronted with a moral decision that could prevent the death of an innocent. Unlike the hypothetical children of Bush's decision, however, Macapagal-Arroyo knew the name of the innocent: Angelo de la Cruz. And Macapagal-Arroyo knew that de la Cruz was a truck driver delivering supplies in Iraq and that he was the father of eight. Philippine officials appealed for de la Cruz's release on the grounds that their presence in Iraq was not as an occupying force. Foreign secretary Delia Albert issued a statement explaining that the function of the Filipino humanitarian group was part of a tradition that had been established years ago to help the Iraqis and that the presence of Filipino civilian workers in Iraq was concrete evidence of the Philippines' commitment to help the people of Iraq restore their sovereignty. Citing the humanitarian assistance provided by Filipino workers, Albert said, "In less than a year of deployment in Iraq, the Philippine humanitarian contingent has constructed 21 schools, 4 footbridges, 3 public health centers, 2 multipurpose halls, repaired 11 water treatment tanks, built 2 kilometers of sewerage systems and asphalted 12 kilometers of road. they conducted 43 medical and civic-action programs, treating more than 14,000 Iraqis and also distributed food and medicine." She added, "Mr. Angelo de la Cruz is part of that tradition. He wishes nothing more than an honest day's wage to feed his wife and 8 young children. He committed no acts of violence against the Iraqi people, nor does he wish them ill."[65]

In July, Macapagal-Arroyo was confronted with a choice that could determine whether one innocent man lived or died. De la Cruz was indeed a civilian, although under a policy of full disclosure (see chapter 2) the government could certainly have made the argument that de la Cruz knew the risks of working in a war torn country. But Macapagal-Arroyo took a different path. Her policies to this point indicated a reluctance to see Filipinos in harm's way. It is important to remember that de la Cruz was not the first Filipino to be taken hostage. And if he had died, he would not have been the first. Weeks earlier, another Filipino truck driver had been gunned down in an ambush. And on those occasions, Macapagal-Arroyo did not withdraw the peacekeeping troops. What was the difference? Cynically (or realistically?), one could argue that Macapagal-Arroyo did not want the blood of de la Cruz on her hands. Alternatively, one could argue that Macapagal-Arroyo was long contemplating a withdrawal of troops. At this point, I favor the latter argument. But why would she consider the removal of peacekeeping forces? Macapagal-Arroyo had, by this point, determined that the War on Terror as it was manifest in Iraq was an unjust war. Angelo de la Cruz would not be sacrificed for an immoral war.

What were the intentions of the United States in going to war against Iraq? And on what moral grounds did Bush have in leading such a war? It is clear now that the Bush administration had no designs to avert war. Indeed, long before the devastation wrought on September 11, 2001, high-ranking officials of the Bush administration were planning on "regime change" in the Middle East. All that was needed was a credible cause. The

War on Terror provided such a justification. Macapagal-Arroyo did not truly support the war against Iraq. Recall from chapter 4 that Macapagal-Arroyo steadfastly avoided the sending of combat troops. And she remained consistent in her attempts to broker a nonmilitarily induced peace in the southern Philippines. According to the Catholic tradition of just war, the pursuit of peace and reconciliation are the only intentions for war. Macapagal-Arroyo, I suggest, reconsidered the intentions of the War on Terror as manifest in the military occupation of Iraq. Why were they there? And for what cause would de la Cruz give his life? Macapagal-Arroyo asked during her 2004 State of the Nation address, "If Angelo de la Cruz had been sacrificed, what would change for the better in Iraq today?"[66] Geopolitically, this is an interesting phrasing in that it underscores her apparent questioning of the continued occupation of Iraq. Macapagal-Arroyo discerned that the paths chosen by the Bush administration did not fit with her goal of peace through development.

A POLITICAL EPILOGUE

In the wake of Macapagal-Arroyo's decision to withdraw the Philippine peacekeeping contingent, Australian prime minister John Howard opined that the Philippine president had made a mistake. He speculated that her actions would not "put the Philippines at any greater immunity from future terrorist attacks." He noted, "The record of al-Qaeda and other organizations is that they hold weakness in contempt, that if people make concessions in the medium- to longer-term they will still pursue those people and they will see them as a softer and more vulnerable target."[67]

The comments of Howard are informative for two reasons. On one hand, Howard associates the Iraqi insurgents with the al-Qaeda organization. However, this association is questionable; indeed, evidence suggests that the entire "linkage" between al-Qaeda and the regime of Saddam Hussein was fabricated in an attempt to justify the U.S.-led war in Iraq. If this is the case, then it is equally erroneous to link postwar events in Iraq with the motivations of al-Qaeda. It is perhaps more plausible to consider the Iraqi insurgents as reacting against what they perceive as an illegal occupation by a colonial power. In a *Foreign Affairs* article written by Larry Diamond, the case is made that the United States gave scant attention to the postwar realities of Iraq. Diamond, who from January to April 2004 served as a senior advisor to the Coalition Provisional Authority in Baghdad, writes, "As a result of a long chain of U.S. miscalculations, the coalition occupation has left

Iraq in far worse shape than it need have and has diminished the long-term prospects of democracy there." Furthermore, he explains that "too many Iraqis viewed the invasion not as an international effort but as an occupation by Western, Christian, essentially Anglo-American powers, and this evoked powerful memories of previous subjugation and of the nationalist struggles against Iraq's former overlords."[68]

Howard's comments are also instructive because they evince a particular understanding of political realism. As indicated earlier, the Bush administration—as well as most politicians—assumed a realist perspective in its approach to international relations. Political realism is grounded in an international politics of sovereign states, all of which attempt to pursue their own interests within context of shifting alliances. With a history of thought stretching back centuries, and including such luminaries as St. Augustine, Machiavelli, Thomas Hobbes, George Kennan, and Henry Kissinger, political realists believe that politics consists of a series of "givens." The first given is the pursuit of power, namely, that in politics people continually try to impose their will on others. This reductionist "crude power politics" is seen, for example, in the geopolitical theories of Friedrick Ratzel in Germany and Kissinger in the United States. A second given is that realists presuppose group loyalty. Accordingly, nationalist discourses are conducive to understandings of realism. States have neither permanent friends nor permanent enemies but, instead, only permanent interests. To the extent that coalitions are formed, these are deemed secondary—and temporary—to the primacy of individual state interests. This accounts for Rumsfeld's "rotating coalitions" as well as the shifts in U.S. support of both Iraq and Iran over the past decades. And a final given is that realists assume that politics are conflictual. War, or at least the threat of war, is therefore central to the realist prescriptions for, and interpretations of, international relations.[69] Within a Hobbesian world, political realists are skeptical of the application of moral concepts such as justice to key problems of foreign policy. Indeed, it is assumed that moral principles obstruct the achievement of sovereign ends. It is significant, of course, that the Bush administration has built a facade of humanitarianism over its realist prescriptions for regime change in Iraq.

Political realists also share a concern with calculating the consequences of actions.[70] In the immediate aftermath of Macapagal-Arroyo's decision to withdraw the Philippines' peacekeeping forces, numerous officials from Australia to the United States warned her of the consequences of such a decision. Powell and Rumsfeld from the United States and Downer from Australia all expressed their concerns that terrorist activities would increase because of the actions of the Philippines. Did Macapagal-Arroyo not consider this possibility? Or were there other more proximate concerns? I return to this briefly. First, however, I recap some of the main issues confronting Macapagal-Arroyo.

Macapagal-Arroyo, in her 2004 address to the Department of Foreign Affairs, accepted full responsibility and made no apologies for her actions. And yet from a realist perspective, her actions do not quite make sense. At the international level, Macapagal-Arroyo risked alienating key players, including the United States and Australia. Conversely, she may have opted to align more closely with her regional neighbors, namely, Indonesia and Malaysia. This decision would most likely reflect a concern that these Islamic Southeast Asian states could better help promote peace and stability in the southern Philippines. In either case, Macapagal-Arroyo would be placed in a difficult position at the international level.

Domestically, does the decision of Macapagal-Arroyo make more sense? Although some analysts indicate that this was the case, I disagree. Macapagal-Arroyo is confronted with two major movements: the CPP–NPA and the Moro Islamic Liberation Front. Not to be discounted, also, is the Abu Sayyaf Group. However, Macapagal-Arroyo is also faced with a fractured government, with many politicians still favoring the ousted former president Joseph Estrada. And not to be forgotten is the position of the Armed Forces of the Philippines. The July 2003 coup attempt was launched in part because of continued support for Estrada. More important, the AFP is also not satisfied with Macapagal-Arroyo's stance on negotiations and military operations. In particular, Macapagal-Arroyo is seen as being too "soft" on terrorism. I maintain that Macapagal-Arroyo's decision may actually foster more motivation for a coup and thus may be seen as politically unwise on the domestic front.

Two months after the de la Cruz incident, twelve Nepalese hostages were killed in Iraq. In response, hundreds of protesters in Katmandu attacked buildings and clashed with police over the executions. Perhaps, therefore, Macapagal-Arroyo secured the release of de la Cruz to prevent the possibility of social unrest in the Philippines. I cannot rule out this possibility. It may very well be that Macapagal-Arroyo was primarily concerned not with simply her political career but the greater possibility of violent protests throughout the Philippines.

Given the importance of overseas employment to the Philippine economy, did Macapagal-Arroyo "spare" the life of de la Cruz to not jeopardize the deployment of future contract workers? This argument is shaky. Historically, when bans have been imposed on the deployment of workers, it has been the workers who rally to lift the ban. Migrant workers from the Philippines, conforming with the "full disclosure" rationale of the government, have tended to accept the conditions of employment abroad. During 2004, it should be remembered, Macapagal-Arroyo had implemented suspensions on the deployment of workers to Iraq. And in August 2004, more than six thousand Filipino workers bound for Iraq appealed to the government to lift the deployment ban. The Philippines stands to lose $102 million in remittances because of the ban. Until Macapagal-Arroyo changes her mind, the ban stays in place. These do not appear to be the actions of a president who is attempting to capitalize on the rebuilding of Iraq.[71] For these same reasons, if Macapagal-Arroyo believed that acquiescence to the terrorists would bring about "immunity" to Filipino workers, why maintain the ban?

So where does this leave the Philippines? From a realist perspective, the decision of Macapagal-Arroyo does not make sense. All in all, there seems to be more negative consequences of the troop withdrawal than there are benefits. Was Macapagal-Arroyo unaware of these consequences? Doubtful. My reading is that Macapagal-Arroyo was clearly aware of these possibilities but that she rejected an ethic of consequences. By upholding the value of an individual life, as opposed to a concern for the greater community of sovereign states, Macapagal-Arroyo appears to have discounted potential consequences of increased violence. Her position conforms more so with an idealist orientation, assuming, for example, that the insurgents are not bent on irrational acts of terror but are attempting to bring about political change (e.g., the end of foreign occupation). Macapagal-Arroyo may have therefore simply discerned that the life of one person outweighed the future risks of the collective and that, more important, one life superceded that of other sovereign states. Her decision thus conforms with an alternative ethics of politics, one that is largely consistent with the teachings of John Paul II and the Catholic church.

In her affirmation of the dignity and the sanctity of the person over that of the state, Macapagal-Arroyo constitutes an alternative to the dominance of political realism. This is only partial, however, in that she does, in other ways, share elements of realism. She speaks of the existence of evil, for example, and of global struggles against not just terrorism but other ills, such as poverty and famine. Adopting a teleological stance, Macapagal-Arroyo views conflict (at times) as inevitable, guided either by the hand of God or "globalization." The difference between Macapagal-Arroyo and the Bush administration lies in the response to these conflicts. For the Philippine president, power is not always met with power; vengeance remains the preserve of the Lord.

How we are to interpret the political fundamentalism of Macapagal-Arroyo is a separate question. The foreign policy of the Philippines between

September 2001 and July 2004 compels us to reconsider our understandings of geopolitics and international relations. The decisions of Macapagal-Arroyo elucidate the importance of theology within foreign policy, and this religiosity is far more substantive than rhetorical theatrics. Discernment, in this case, is a practice of the Philippines' foreign policy.

Peter Singer, in his study of the ethics of Bush, writes, "Whether he believes in the fine phrases and lofty rhetoric that he uses, or is consciously using it to win public support, it is clear that Bush has no real interest in the policy details needed to achieve the aspirations he has voiced. He has failed to follow through on most of the commitments he has made to work for a better, more just society. . . . Rather than ensure that the nation he leads is a good global citizen, Bush has spurned institutions for global cooperation and set back the task of making the rule of law, rather than force, the determining factor in world affairs." Singer concludes that, ultimately, "it is impossible to be sure how genuine Bush and those who advise him are about the ethics that he advocates."[72] In like fashion, it is unclear at this point whether the morality evinced by Macapagal-Arroyo was "real" or simply a political ploy to achieve some as yet unspecified objective. I have argued, however, that the totality of Macapagal-Arroyo's actions leading to and following the decision to secure the release of de la Cruz was consistent in her ethical stance. Consequently, we should not consider her decision in the de la Cruz incident in isolation but rather as one element in her overall approach to foreign policy.

Derek Gregory writes that the task of a critical human geography—of a geographical imagination—is to recognize the corporeality of vision and reach out, from one body to another, not in a mood of arrogance, aggression, and conquest but in a spirit of humility, understanding, and care.[73] Perhaps history will remember the actions of Macapagal-Arroyo as one hopeful offering of peace in a violent time.

NOTES

1. Ma. Theresa Torres, "Filipino Hostage in Iraq," *Manila Times*, July 9, 2004, www.manilatimes.net/national/2004/jul/09/yehey/top_stories/20040709top1.html (July 16, 2004).

2. Neil Villegas Mugas and Maricel Cruz, "GMA Directs DFA to Ensure Pinoy's Safety in War-Torn Iraq," *Manila Times*, April 14, 2004, www.manilatimes.net/national/2004/apr/14/yehey/top_stories/20040414top9.html (April 13, 2004).

3. Ma. Theresa Torres and Efren Danao, "Sending of Workers to Iraq Suspended," *Manila Times*, July 9, 2004, www.manilatimes.net/national/2004/jul/09/yehey/top_stories/20040709top4.html (July 16, 2004).

4. Jowie Corpuz, "Race against Time to Free De La Cruz," *Manila Times*, July 10, 2004, www.manilatimes.net/national/2004/jul/10/yehey/top_stories/2004 0710top1.html (July 16, 2004).

5. Wire report, "Last Plea from Angelo," *Manila Times*, July 11, 2004, www.manilatimes.net/national/2004/jul/11/yehey/top_stories/20040711top1.html (July 16, 2004).

6. Wire report, "UN's Annan Joins Plea to Save Angelo," *Manila Times*, July 11, 2004, www.manilatimes.net/national/2004/jul/11/yehey/top_stories/20040711 top2.html (July 16, 2004).

7. Wire report, "Cimatu Taps Iraqi Negotiators," *Manila Times*, July 11, 2004, www.manilatimes.net/national/2004/jul/11/yehey/top stories/20040711top3 .html (July 16, 2004).

8. Karl Kaufman, "NPA: Gloria Will Pay If Hostage Dies," *Manila Times*, July 11, 2004, www.manilatimes.net/national/2004/jul/11/yehey/top_stories/2004 0711top4.html (July 16, 2004).

9. Neil Villegas Mugas, "Clamor for Iraq Pullout Gets Louder," *Manila Times*, July 12, 2004, www.manilatimes.net/national/2004/jul/11/yehey/top_stories/ 20040712top5.html (July 16, 2004).

10. Ma. Theresa Torres, "Angelo Is Given a 9-Day Reprieve," *Manila Times*, July 12, 2004, www.manilatimes.net/national/2004/jul/12/yehey/top_stories/2004 0712top1.html (July 16, 2004).

11. Ma. Theresa Torres, "Iraqi Militants Reject Ransom," *Manila Times*, July 12, 2004, www.manilatimes.net/national/2004/jul/13/yehey/top_stories/20040713 top1.html (July 16, 2004). It is too early to fully understand the negotiations that took place behind closed doors. Further research will no doubt uncover, through written sources and interviews, something of the atmosphere and potential differences of opinion within the Macapagal-Arroyo administration. Likewise, the premature comments by Sto. Tomas, current labor secretary and former head of the Philippine Overseas Employment Administration, warrant closer scrutiny.

12. Max de Leon, "RP Business Deal with Iraq Remains Strong—Romulo," *Manila Times*, July 13, 2004, www.manilatimes.net/national/2004/jul/13/yehey/ top_stories/20040713top8.html (July 16, 2004).

13. Torres, "Militants Reject Ransom."

14. Florante Solmerin, "Government Handling of Hostage Crisis May Imperil Peace Talks—NDF," *Manila Times*, July 13, 2004, www.manilatimes.net/national/ 2004/jul/13/yehey/prov/20040713pro1.html (August 4, 2004).

15. It was later revealed that at the time of the crisis, the Philippines only had a contingent of forty-three persons, not the reported fifty-one. According to officials of the Department of Foreign Affairs, the Philippine government agreed to

"send home" eight soldiers in compliance with the demand of de la Cruz's captors to remove the peacekeeping forces. At the time, however, these eight soldiers were already in Manila. Apparently the Philippine government "lied" to the abductors in an attempt to gain more time for de la Cruz. See Jowie Corpuz, "DFA 'Lied' to Save Angelo from Death," *Manila Times*, July 24, 2004, www.manila times.net/national/2004/jul/24/yehey/top_stories/20040724top6.html (July 26, 2004).

16. Jowie Corpuz, "I'm Coming Back Home," *Manila Times*, July 16, 2004, www .manilatimes.net/national/2004/jul/16/yehey/top_stories/20040716top1.html (July 16, 2004).

17. Jowie Corpuz and Ma. Theresa Torres, "Rumsfeld Scores Manila's 'Weakness,'" *Manila Times*, July 23, 2004, www.manilatimes.net/national/2004/jul/23/yehey/top_stories/20040723top2.html (July 26, 2004).

18. Marichu Villanueva, "President Arroyo: Hostage Crisis My Defining Moment!" *Philippine Headline News Online*, July 24, 2004, www.newsflash.org/2004/02/pe/pe003396.htm (August 20, 2004).

19. Jowie Corpuz, "Pullout Dismays US, Other Allies," *Manila Times*, July 15, 2004, www.manilatimes.net/national/2004/jul/15/yehey/top_stories/20040715 top2.html (August 4, 2004).

20. Karl Kaufman, "Ricciardone: US, RP Remain Allies," *Manila Times*, July 16, 2004, www.manilatimes.net/national/2004/jul/16/yehey/top_stories/20040716 top3.html (July 16, 2004).

21. Wire reports, "Powell, White House Join Rebuke," *Manila Times*, July 17, 2004, www.manilatimes.net/national/2004/jul/17/yehey/top_stories/20040717 top2.html (July 19, 2004).

22. Jowie Corpuz, "Singapore Joins RP Bashers; DFA Mum," *Manila Times*, August 4, 2004, www.manilatimes.net/national/2004/aug/04/yehey/top_stories/20040804top2.html (August 3, 2004).

23. Corpuz, "Pullout Dismays US."

24. Corpuz, "Singapore Joins."

25. Wire reports, "Powell, White House."

26. In September these seven men were released unharmed. See Bassen Mroue, "Kidnappers in Iraq Free Seven Truckers," *Yahoo! News*, September 1, 2004, http://news.yahoo.com/news/ (September 1, 2004).

27. Associated Foreign Press, "Iraqi Hostage-Takers Seize 7 Truck Drivers," *Manila Times*, July 23, 2004, www.manilatimes.net/national/2004/jul/23/yehey/top_stories/20040723top3.html (August 4, 2004).

28. Associated Press, "Egyptian First Envoy Abducted in Baghdad," *Manila Times*, July 25, 2004, www.manilatimes.net/national/2004/jul/25/yehey/top_stories/20040725top3.html (July 26, 2004).

29. Jowie Corpuz, "Australia Blames RP, Spain for Terror Threat," *Manila Times*, July 26, 2004, www.manilatimes.net/national/2004/jul/26/yehey/top_stories/20040726top6.html (July 26, 2004).

30. Wire report, "Angelo Safety Comes First," *Manila Times*, July 18, 2004, www.manilatimes.net/national/2004/jul/18/yehey/top_stories/20040718top1.html (July 19, 2004).

31. Anthony Vargas, "NPA Sets Terms for Soldiers' Release," *Manila Times*, July 19, 2004, www.manilatimes.net/national/2004/jul/19/yehey/top_stories/20040719 top4.html (August 4, 2004).

32. Karl Kaufman, "Military Turns Down SOMO for Release of Hostaged Soldiers," *Manila Times*, July 20, 2004, www.manilatimes.net/national/2004/jul/20/yehey/top_stories/20040720top7.html (August 4, 2004).

33. Armand Galang, "Army Sergeant Shot Dead by NPA Hitman in Ecija," *Manila Times*, July 18, 2004, www.manilatimes.net/national/2004/jul/18/yehey/prov/20040718pro2.html (August 4, 2004).

34. Wire report, "Palace Lashes Back at Ricciardone for 'Dictating,'" *Manila Times*, July 8, 2004, www.manilatimes.net/national/2004/jul/08/yehey/top_stories/20040708top6.html (July 16, 2004).

35. Sammy Martin, "Pimentel Wants US in on GRP-MILF Peace Talks," *Manila Times*, July 9, 2004, www.manilatimes.net/national/2004/jul/09/yehey/top_stories/20040709top9.html (August 3, 2004).

36. Sammy Martin, "Mend Strained Ties with US, Pimentel Urges Arroyo Govt," *Manila Times*, July 24, 2004, www.manilatimes.net/national/2004/jul/24/yehey/top_stories/20040724top11.html (July 26, 2004).

37. Associated Foreign Press, "JI Training New Terrorists in RP—Report," *Manila Times*, July 14, 2004, www.manilatimes.net/national/2004/jul/14/yehey/top_stories/20040714top1.html (August 3, 2004).

38. Jowie Corpuz, "Washington: Terror Threat 'Greatest' in RP, Indonesia," *Manila Times*, October 18, 2003, www.manilatimes.net/national/2001/oct/18/top_stories/20031018top8.html (March 26, 2004).

39. Marichu Villanueva, "Arroyo Disputes US Terror Risk Tag," *Philippine Star*, November 6, 2003, www.philstar.com/philstar (November 14, 2003).

40. Jowie Corpuz, "Study: RP on 'High-Risk' List of Terrorism Targets," *Manila Times*, February 24, 2004, www.manilatimes.net/2004/feb/24/yehey/metro/20040224met5.html (March 26, 2004).

41. Office of the Press Secretary, "State of the Union Address," www.white house.gov/news/releases/2004/01/print/20040120-7.html (March 31, 2004).

42. Neil Villegas Mugas, "US 'Diplomatic Reproach' Fictitious, Says President," *Manila Times*, April 13, 2004, www.manilatimes.net/2004/apr/13/yehey/top_stories/20040413top6.html (April 12, 2004).

43. Karl Kaufman, "Feliciano Report 'Clears' AFP," *Manila Times*, October 19, 2003, www.manilatimes.net/national/2003/oct/19/top_stories/20031019top8.html (August 3, 2004).

44. Office of the President, "PGMA's Speech during the Department of Foreign Affairs (DFA) Foundation Day 2004" July 23, 2004, www.ops.gov.ph/speeches 2004/speech-2004july23.htm (August 9, 2004).

45. Office of the President, "Foundation Day Speech."

46. Office of the President, "PGMA's Speech during the Memorial Mass for the Victims of the September 11, 2001, Tragedy," November 18, 2001, www.opnet.ops .gov.ph/speech-2001nov18.htm (August 23, 2004).

47. Office of the President, "PGMA's Speech during the 21st National Prayer Breakfast," August 16, 2001, www.opnet.ops.gov.ph/speech-2001aug15.htm (August 23, 2004).

48. Office of the President, "21st National Prayer Breakfast."

49. Office of the President, "PGMA's Speech during the 21st Bishops-Ulama Conference and General Assembly and Asian Gathering of Muslim Ulama and Christian Bishops," August 18, 2003, www.ops.gov.ph/speeches2003/speech-2003 aug18.htm (August 23, 2004).

50. Office of the President, "Foundation Day Speech."

51. Office of the President, "Statement of the President on Her Holy Week Message," April 5, 2004, www.ops.gov.ph/speeches2004/speech-2004apr05.htm (August 23, 2004).

52. Office of the President, "PGMA's Speech during the 22nd Philippines National Prayer Breakfast," November 12, 2003, www.ops.gov.ph/speeches2003/ speech-2003nov12.htm (August 23, 2004).

53. Danny Morris and Charles Olsen, *Discerning God's Will Together: A Spiritual Practice for the Church* (Nashville, Tenn.: Upper Room Books, 1997), 24.

54. Office of the President, "22nd National Prayer Breakfast."

55. Peter Singer, *The President of Good and Evil: The Ethics of George W. Bush* (New York: Dutton, 2004), 156–60.

56. Larry Everest, *Oil, Power, and Empire: Iraq and the U.S. Global Agenda* (Monroe, Maine: Common Courage Press, 2004), 8–9.

57. Richard Falk, *The Great Terror War* (New York: Olive Branch Press, 2003), 3.

58. Office of the President, "Her Excellency President Gloria Macapagal-Arroyo State of the Nation Address," July 26, 2004, www.op.gov.ph/speeches/ (July 26, 2004).

59. Derek S. Jeffreys, *Defending Human Dignity: John Paul II and Political Realism* (Grand Rapids, Mich.: Brazos Press, 2004).

60. Villanueva, "Defining Moment."

61. Office of the President, "Release of Angelo de la Cruz," July 19–25, 2004, www.op.gov.ph/pms/currentissues.asp?action=view&id=2641 (July 29, 2004).

62. Villanueva, "Defining Moment."

63. Michael Walzer, *Just and Unjust Wars: A Moral Argument with Historical Illustrations* (New York: Basic Books, 1977), 136.

64. Singer, *President of Good and Evil*, 158.

65. Wire report, "Annan Joins Plea."

66. Office of the President, "2004 State of the Nation Address."

67. Wire Report, "Australia Slams Arroyo for Appeasing Terrorists," *Manila Bulletin*, July 21, 2004, www.mb.com.ph/issues/2004/07/21/MAIN2004072114539_ print.html (July 29, 2004).

68. Larry Diamond, "What Went Wrong in Iraq," *Foreign Affairs* 83 (2004): 34–56 (quotes on 34 and 43).

69. Jeffreys, *Defending Human Dignity*, 14–15; Peter J. Taylor and Colin Flint, *Political Geography: World-Economy, Nation-State, and Locality*, 4th ed. (New York: Prentice Hall, 2000), 52.

70. Jeffreys, *Defending Human Dignity*, 16.

71. Jowie Corpuz, "Ban on OFW Deployment in Iraq Stays, Says Cimatu," *Manila Times*, August 4, 2004, www.manilatimes.net/national/2004/aug/04/yehey/top_stories/20040804top11.html (August 3, 2004).

72. Singer, *President of Good and Evil*, 224–25.

73. Derek Gregory, *Geographical Imaginations* (Cambridge, Mass.: Blackwell, 1994), 416.

SELECTED BIBLIOGRAPHY

Anderson, Sarah, Phyllis Bennis, and John Cavanagh. "Coalition of the Willing or Coalition of the Coerced? How the Bush Administration Influences Allies in Its War on Iraq." Institute for Policy Studies, 2004, www.ips-dc.org (August 22, 2004).

Asis, Maruja M. B. "The Overseas Employment Program Policy." In *Philippine Labour Migration: Impact and Policy*, edited by G. Battistella and A. Paganoni, 68–112. Quezon City, Philippines: Scalabrini Migration Center, 1992.

Ball, Rochelle, and Nicola Piper. "Globalisation and Regulation of Citizenship— Filipino Migrant Workers in Japan." *Political Geography* 21 (2002): 1013–34.

Belkeziz, Abdelouahed. "Speech of H. E. Dr. Abdelouahed Belkeziz, the Secretary-General of the Organization of the Islamic Conference, at the Inauguration of the Tenth Session of the Islamic Summit Conference." Organization of Islamic Conference, 2003, www.oic-oci-org/press/english/october2004/sg10summit.htm (August 19, 2004).

Bello, Walden, D. Kinley, and E. Elinson. *Development Debacle: The World Bank in the Philippines*. San Francisco: Institute for Food and Development Policy, 1982.

Bennis, Phyllis. *Before and After: U.S. Foreign Policy and the War on Terror*. New York: Olive Branch Press, 2003.

Bos, Stefan J. "Philippines President Arroyo Says God Told Her Not to Run in Next Election." Bible Network News, 2002, www.biblenetworknews.com/asiapacific/ 123002_philippines.html (August 9, 2004).

Calinicos, Alex. *The New Mandarins of American Power*. Cambridge: Polity Press, 2003.

Casco, Richard R. *Full Disclosure Policy: A Philosophical Orientation*. Manila: Philippine Overseas Employment Administration, 1995.

———. *Managing International Labour Migration and the Framework for the Deregulation of the POEA*. Manila: Philippine Overseas Employment Administration, 1997.

Cooley, John. *Unholy Wars: Afghanistan, America, and International Terrorism*. London: Pluto Press, 2002.

Daalder, Ivo H., and James M. Lindsay. *America Unbound: The Bush Revolution in Foreign Policy.* Washington, D.C.: Brookings Institution, 2003.

Darsey, James F. *The Prophetic Tradition and Radical Rhetoric in America* New York: New York University Press, 1997.

Diamond, Larry. "What Went Wrong in Iraq?" *Foreign Affairs* 83 (2004): 34–56.

Domke, David. *God Willing? Political Fundamentalism in the White House, the "War on Terror," and the Echoing Press.* London: Pluto Press, 2004.

Edelman, Murray. *Political Language: Words That Succeed and Politics That Fail.* New York: Academic Press, 1977.

Edkins, Jenny. *Poststructuralism and International Relations: Bringing the Political Back In.* Boulder, Colo.: Lynne Rienner, 1999.

Elshtain, Jean Bethke. *Just War against Terror: The Burden of American Power in a Violent World.* New York: Basic Books, 2003.

Everest, Larry. *Oil, Power, and Empire: Iraq and the U.S. Global Agenda.* Monroe, Maine: Common Courage Press, 2003.

Falk, Richard. *The Great Terror War.* New York: Olive Branch Press, 2003.

Foucault, Michel. "Truth and Power." In *Power/Knowledge: Selected Interviews and Other Writings, 1972–1977,* edited by C. Gordon, trans. C. Gordon, L. Marshall, J. Mepham, and K. Soper, 109–33. New York: Pantheon Books, 1980.

Freedman, Lawrence, and Efraim Karsh. *The Gulf Conflict 1990–1991: Diplomacy and War in the New World Order.* Princeton, N.J.: Princeton University Press, 1993.

Garmone, Jim. "Coalition of the Willing Provides Formidable Force." American Forces Press Service, March 19, 2003, www.q77.com/iraqwar/afpnews/afp182 .htm (August 22, 2004).

Gonzalez, Juan L. *Philippine Labour Migration: Critical Dimensions of Public Policy.* Singapore: Institute of Southeast Asian Studies, 1998.

Gregory, Derek. *Geographical Imaginations.* Cambridge, Mass.: Blackwell, 1994.

Harding, Jim. *After Iraq: War, Imperialism, and Democracy.* London: Merlin Press, 2004.

Harvey, David. *The New Imperialism.* Oxford: Oxford University Press, 2003.

———. *Spaces of Hope.* Berkeley: University of California Press, 2000.

Hawes, Gary. *The Philippine State and the Marcos Regime: The Politics of Export.* Ithaca, N.Y.: Cornell University Press, 1987.

Howard-Pitney, David. *The Afro-American Jeremiad: Appeals for Justice in America.* Philadelphia: Temple University Press, 1990.

Jeffreys, Derek S. *Defending Human Dignity: John Paul II and Political Realism.* Grand Rapids, Mich.: Brazos Press, 2004.

Johnson, Chalmers. *The Sorrows of Empire: Militarism, Secrecy, and the End of the Republic.* New York: Henry Holt, 2004.

Karnow, Stanley. *In Our Image: America's Empire in the Philippines.* New York: Random House, 1989.

Kellner, Douglas. *From 9/11 to Terror War: The Dangers of the Bush Legacy.* Lanham, Md.: Rowman & Littlefield, 2003.

Kelly, Philip F. "Globalization, Power, and the Politics of Scale in the Philippines." *Geoforum* 28 (1997): 151–71.

———. *Landscapes of Globalization: Human Geographies of Economic Change in the Philippines*. London: Routledge, 2000.

Kho, Madge. "A Conflict That Won't Go Away," www.philippineupdate.com/Conflict.htm (September 2, 2002).

Kuruvill, S. "Economic Development Strategies, Industrial Relations Policies, and Workplace IR/HR Practices in Southeast Asia." In *The Comparative Political Economy of Industrial Relations*, edited by K. Wever and L. Turner, 115–50. Madison: Industrial Relations Research Association Series, University of Wisconsin, 1995.

Linn, Brian M. *The Philippine War, 1899–1902*. Lawrence: University of Kansas Press, 2000.

Manila Bulletin, www.mb.com.ph.

Manila Times, www.manilatimes.net.

Mann, Michael. *Incoherent Empire*. New York: Verso, 2003.

May, R. J. "The Domestic in Foreign Policy: The Flor Contemplacion Case and Philippine–Singapore Relations." *Pilipinas* 29 (1997): 63–76.

McKenna, Thomas M. *Muslim Rulers and Rebels: Everyday Politics and Armed Separatism in the Southern Philippines*. Berkeley: University of California Press, 1998.

Morris, Danny, and Charles Olsen. *Discerning God's Will Together: A Spiritual Practice for the Church*. Nashville, Tenn.: Upper Room Books, 1997.

National Economic Development Authority. *The Medium-Term Philippine Development Plan, 2001–2004, with the 2001 State of the Nation Address*. Manila: National Economic Development Authority, 2001.

Nolledo, J. N., ed. *The Labor Code of the Philippines, with Implementing Regulations, Related Laws, and Other Issuances*. Manila: National Bookstore, 1993.

Office of the Philippine President, www.ops.gov.ph, January 2001–August 2004.

Office of the Press Secretary, www.whitehouse.gov, September 2001–August 2004.

Overholt, William H. "Pressures and Policies: Prospects for Cory Aquino's Philippines." In *Rebuilding a Nation: Philippine Challenges and American Policy*, edited by Carl H. Lande, 89–110. Washington, D.C.: Washington Institute Press, 1987.

Philippine Overseas Employment Administration. "Market Development: Seeking Purpose and Promise for Filipino Skills." *Overseas Employment Info Series* 1 (1988): 5–9.

———. *Migrant Workers and Overseas Filipinos Act of 1995: Republic Act 8042 and Its Implementing Rules and Regulations*. Manila: Department of Labor and Employment, 1996.

Philippine Star, www.philstar/philstar.

Prestowitz, Clyde. *Rogue Nation: American Unilateralism and the Failure of Good Intentions*. New York: Basic Books, 2003.

Rice, Condoleeza. "Campaign 2000—Promoting the National Interest." *Foreign Affairs* 79 (2000), www.foreignpolicy2000.org/library/issuebriefs/readingnotes/fa_rice.html (July 28, 2004).

Simons, Geoff. *Iraq: From Sumer to Post-Saddam*. New York: Palgrave MacMillam, 2004.

Singer, Peter. *The President of Good and Evil: The Ethics of George W. Bush*. New York: Dutton, 2004.

Stahl, Charles W. *International Labor Migration: A Study of the ASEAN Countries*. New York: Center for Migration Studies, 1986.

Steinberg, David J. *The Philippines: A Singular and a Plural Place*, 3rd ed. Boulder, Colo.: Westview Press, 1994.

Taylor, Peter J., and Colin Flint. *Political Geography: World-Economy, Nation-State, and Locality*, 4th ed. New York: Prentice Hall, 2000.

Timberman, David G. *A Changeless Land: Continuity and Change in Philippine Politics*. New York: M. E. Sharpe, 1991.

Tyner, James A. *Made in the Philippines: Gendered Discourses and the Making of Migrants*. London: Routledge, 2004.

———. "Migrant Labour and the Politics of Scale: Gendering the Philippine State." *Asia Pacific Viewpoint* 41 (2000): 131–54.

———. "The Spatial Structure of the Philippines' Overseas Employment Program." *Asian Geographer* 19 (2000): 139–56.

United States Institute of Peace. "Special Report 69: Catholic Contributions to International Peace." United States Institute of Peace, www.usip.org/pubs/special reports/sr69.html (August 9, 2004).

Villegas, E. M. *The Political Economy of Philippine Labor Laws*. Quezon City, Philippines: Foundation for Nationalist Studies, 1988.

Walzer, Michael. *Just and Unjust Wars: A Moral Argument with Historical Illustrations*. New York: Basic Books, 1977.

Welch, Richard E. *Response to Imperialism: The United States and the Philippine–American War, 1899–1902*. Chapel Hill: University of North Carolina Press, 1979.

Woodiwiss, Anthony. *Globalisation, Human Rights, and Labour Law in Pacific Asia*. Cambridge: Cambridge University Press, 1998.

Woodward, Peter N. *Oil and Labor in the Middle East: Saudi Arabia and the Oil Boom*. New York: Praeger, 1988.

INDEX

ABOUT THE AUTHOR

James A. Tyner is associate professor of geography at Kent State University. He received his PhD in geography from the University of Southern California. He has written extensively on the subjects of migration and the Philippines and is the author of *Made in the Philippines: Gendered Discourses and the Making of Migrations*. He currently lives in northeast Ohio with his wife, Belinda, and their daughter, Jessica.